Pattern Design for Children's Clothes

Pattern Design for Children's Clothes

Gloria Mortimer-Dunn

B T Batsford Ltd, London

© Gloria Mortimer-Dunn 1993, 1996
First edition published 1993
This edition published 1996

Printed in Great Britain by Butler and Tanner.

Published by
B T Batsford Ltd
4 Fitzhardinge Street
London W1H 0AH

A CIP catalogue record for this book is available from
the British Library.

ISBN 0 7134 7874 8

Contents

Designing for children

The constantly changing face of fashion is a reflection of social and technical development. Clothing for girls and boys must always be practical, comfortable to wear and easy to care for. The garments should be very simple and far less intricate in design than those for adults. Garments must be loose to avoid restricting the movement of an active child.

Nowadays there is no reason to clothe a child as a miniature adult because there is sufficient variety in colour, fabric and design to dress children in a manner more suitable to their age group.

There are no rules for designing for children as adult fashion trends can be easily adapted. Simplicity is the key to good design. Avoid breaking up the basic shape and keep detail to a minimum. Watch the proportions of the figure and avoid the distortion of a badly placed design or seam line or the incorrect positioning of the pockets or contrast colour bands.

Consider the method of fastening and make it easy for young children to dress themselves. Elasticated waistlines on trousers, shorts and skirts will enable these garments to be pulled on. Ensure the necklines of tops are large enough to be pulled easily over the head. Front buttoning and zippers make it simple for young fingers to manage dressing.

Choose loose fitting garments, be they tops, trousers, shorts, skirts, overalls, tracksuits or dresses. Trapeze and A-line dresses are ideal for girls as they allow for natural growth and do not constrict across the chest or around a rising waistline.

Rely on colour, fabric and prints to give interest to the clothing. Most colour schemes are now acceptable for children of either sex. Fashion dictates the new season's colour story which is then reflected in many ranges of fabrics, garments and accessories. Use colour to advantage, be it solid, monotone, soft pastels, deep, rich colours or brilliant primaries grouped as harmonies or clashing in a riot of multi-colours. Fabrics such as sailcloth, twill, cord and denims supply tough-wearing play clothes for girls and boys alike. Synthetic and blended fabrics are ideal for general wear because they require minimum care and little or no ironing. Knitted fabrics give more freedom of movement than woven fabrics and are ideal for casual wear.

Special occasion garments such as formal and party wear can indulge in more impractical fabrics and styling.

Remember to keep the styling simple when designing for children. Simplicity will always give the best results.

Pattern design

Pattern Design for Children's Clothes introduces a systematic method of making patterns from which any design can be cut.

The basic 'block' or master patterns can be made from the basic block pattern drafts in this book or taken from commercial paper patterns. The block can even be cut from patterns made from fabric fitted on the figure. Once the blocks have been established, then the creation of all other patterns can begin.

An essential part of creating fashion is the ability to make the patterns from which the garments are cut. To do this successfully, basic principles of the figure, shape, proportions and design must be understood. The secret of good patternmaking is to be versatile and to be able to manipulate basic patterns. All that is needed is common sense and, with experience, practice makes perfect.

A system of children's sizes has been universally accepted by most manufacturers. The system considers height the most reliable indication of size, followed by chest measurement. Age is not considered a reliable guide due to variations in the growth rate.

These block draft patterns are designed to fit the average child's figure only. No allowance has been made in the larger size block patterns for early puberty in girls.

Children grow at different rates, but the average child grows approximately a size each year with a height increase of about 6cm (21/2").

The chest measurement increases about 2cm (3/4") from 2 to 6 year olds with an increase of 3cm (11/4") for 8 to 14-year-old girls and boys.

Small children tend to have prominent stomachs and these have been allowed for in the block draft patterns. As children grow, there is a more pronounced difference between the waist and hip measurements in the larger sizes.

Construction of the basic block draft patterns

The basic block patterns are the foundation from which other garment patterns are constructed. These draft patterns become the 'block' or master patterns from which all the following patterns are derived. Block patterns are never cut, slashed or mutilated in any way, but tracings are made from them. When tracing around a block draft, remember to add seam allowance to any new seam edges.

As block patterns are in constant use, it is advisable to ensure that they are cut out of a heavy pattern paper or cardboard. It is essential that the block patterns are immediately replaced when edges show sign of wear. Inaccurate fit and distortion can result from using tattered and repaired patterns. For greater accuracy, always re-cut the block patterns from the basic draft and not by tracing around the old patterns.

In manufacturing, the block patterns are made in a sample size only: usually in size 6 for children and size 10 for girls and boys. It is from these sample size patterns that the complete size range is developed.

This is done by grading the pattern down for smaller sizes and up for the larger sizes. This term 'grading' means the proportional increase or decrease of the sample size pattern according to the standard body measurements.

Grading saves drafting different patterns for each size. A dressmaker can use this method to advantage when adapting fashion designs to different figure types and sizes.

Any good commercial printed paper pattern can be used as a block pattern and this eliminates drafting. Transfer the pattern to heavy paper or cardboard before using it in the usual way.

Throughout this book many patterns are shown as 'half' patterns where the centre line is placed on the fold as the pattern is the same on each side. This occurs in the basic bodice and skirt block drafts and other patterns. For manufacturing, these patterns must be traced off and a 'full' pattern made prior to cutting out the fabric. Dressmakers can use the 'half' pattern by placing the centre line on the fold of the fabric.

When a pattern is different on each side a full pattern must be made. A sleeve pattern is a good example of a full pattern which is different on each side of the head or crown shaping.

Measurements

Accurate measurements are essential for the successful fit of any garment. It is important that they are taken in the correct position as shown on the standard body measurement chart. This is particularly important when preparing patterns for manufacturing because inaccurate patterns not only waste time and money but result in badly fitting clothes.

The measurements given are based on those of the average child and are similar to those measurements used for commercial printed paper patterns and by garment manufacturers. They should fit the majority of figures in any size group.

These are body measurements and have been taken over clothing with no ease of movement allowed.

This ease has been included in the construction of all the basic block draft patterns.

8cm (31/8") ease is added to the chest measurement.
4cm (11/2") ease is added to the waist measurement.
6cm (21/2") ease is added to the hip measurement.
2cm (3/4") ease is added to the sleeve head for sizes 8-10-12-14.

All the basic block draft patterns are for woven fabrics. If using knitted fabric, then this amount of ease must be reduced depending on the amount of stretch in the fabric.

Fitting

Couture houses are renowned for the superb fit of their garments which is achieved by taking several fittings. In manufacturing, the fitting is done on the 'pilot' or sample garment and any alteration is done to the pattern prior to grading for the different sizes.

The home dressmaker should first cut the block pattern out of the 'mull' or a muslin, lawn or calico fabric for a fitting. This is called a 'toile'. The block pattern can then be adjusted if necessary. This is helpful when making patterns for a child who is not quite the average figure or if the garment design is complicated.

Tools of the trade

Tools for patternmaking should be of good quality and accurate design to achieve the best results. The following list can be used as a guide and be added to as required.

All tools must be replaced when they show signs of wear.

1. A fibreglass tape measure is the best as one made from cotton will stretch with use and become inaccurate.

2. A metric ruler for drafting, patternmaking and measuring fabric.

3. A graduated square ruler, preferably with a reinforced metal corner for strength.

4. A parallel ruler assists in the grading of patterns for manufacturing purposes.

5. Hard grade pencils, 2H to 4H, are best for accuracy in patternmaking.

6. Broad-tipped marking pens to mark both sides of the pattern with essential information such as fabric grain lines, garment size, style number, number of pieces to be cut from each pattern piece, type of fabric and any other relevant details.

7. Chalk is useful for marking around patterns placed on the fabric, alterations to the fit of the garment and marking the level of a hem.

8. Shears must be sharp to cut fabric. Reserve another pair for cutting paper or cardboard as these will blunt quickly.

9. A tracing wheel with clear, spiked points is most useful.

10. A pattern notcher for making corresponding balance marks on the pattern is necessary for manufacturing purposes.

11. A stiletto or bradawl point for perforating patterns to mark the end of darts, pocket placement and the positions of button and buttonholes on the patterns.
A small hand punch is generally used in manufacturing.

12. A stapler for joining pieces of pattern together to prevent slipping when cutting more than once piece of pattern at the same time.

13. Good quality pattern paper or cardboard must be used for all patterns, especially for basic block patterns. This is essential for manufacturing.

14. A supply of 'mull' calico, lawn or sheeting is useful to fit the basic block drafts and to make 'toiles' or trial garments of more complicated styles.

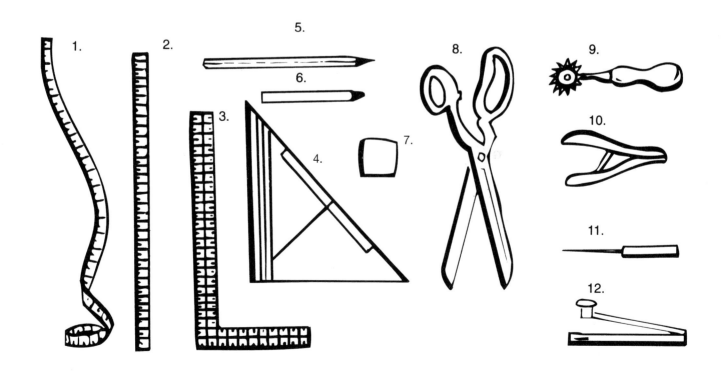

Standard body measurement chart

Accurate measurements are essential for the successful fit of any garment. It is important that they are taken in the correct position as shown on the standard body measurement chart.

These measurements are used throughout the book for both the construction of the basic block draft and other pattern designs.

The measurements are based on the standard figure. They are used by manufacturing and commercial paper pattern companies.

Personal measurements can be substituted for those given below.

The measurements below have been taken over clothing. They are not garment measurements and do not include ease of movement. The required ease has been added to the basic block draft patterns.

For imperial version see p82.

	Children			Girls & Boys				Centimetres
Sizes	2	4	6	8	10	12	14	
1. Approximate age	2	4	6	8	10	12	14	Years
2. Height	92	106	120	130	140	150	160	Taken vertically from the crown of the head to the floor.
3. Chest	56	60	64	68	72	76	80	Taken around the body at the fullest part of the chest over the shoulder blades.
4. Waist	54	56	58	60	62	64	66	A comfortable measurement taken at the waistline.
5. Hips	56	61	66	72	78	84	90	Taken at the fullest part of the hipline.
6. Centre front	19	21	23	25	27.5	30	32.5	From base of front neck to waistline.
7. Across front	22	23	24	27	28.5	30	31.5	Approximately midway between the top and bottom of the armhole.
8. Centre back	23.5	25.5	27.5	29.5	32	34.5	37	From nape of back neck to waistline.
9. Across back	23	24	25	28	29.5	31	32.5	Over the shoulder blades, approximately midway between top and bottom of armhole.
10. Side seam	9	10.5	12	13.5	15	16.5	18	Up from waistline to approximately 2.5cm below armpit.
11. Neck circumference	25	27	29	31	33	35	37	A loose measurement taken at the base of the neck.
12. Shoulder	7	7.5	8	9	9.5	10	10.5	From base of side neck to the shoulder point.
13. Overarm	36	42	48	54	60	66	72	From base of side neck to wrist with the arm bent.
14. Underarm	24	27	30	33	35	37	39	From the armhole to the wrist.
15. Upper arm	18	19	20	22	23	24	25	At fullest part of the bicep.
16. Body rise or crotch depth	20	22	24	26	27	28	29	Taken seated and measured from the side waist to the seat, plus 2.5cm.
17. Waist to hip	10	12	14	16	16	17	18	From centre back waist to fullest part of the hipline.
18. Waist to knee	35	40	45	50	55	60	65	Taken from back waist to back of knee.
19. Waist height	56	64	72	80	88	96	104	From back waist to floor.

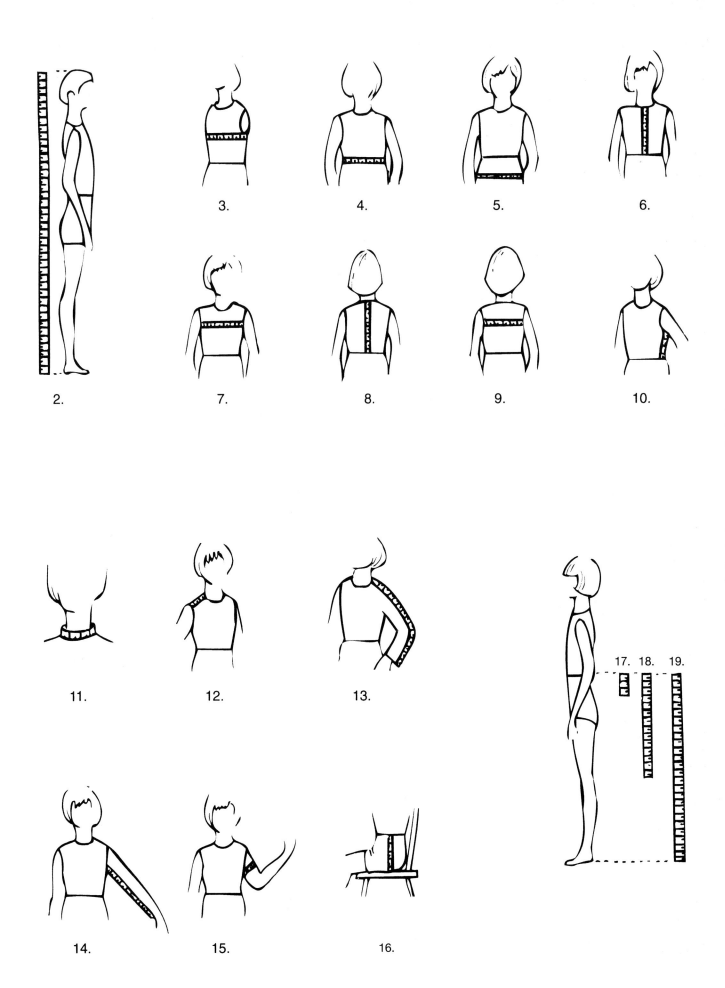

2.

3.

4.

5.

6.

7.

8.

9.

10.

11.

12.

13.

17. 18. 19.

14.

15.

16.

Fabric preparation

Choosing the fabric

Great care must be taken to choose the most suitable fabric for the style. Remember that the more complicated the design, the plainer the fabric must be. It is advisable to choose a solid coloured fabric for any style with many seams, darts and pockets as a plain material will not detract from these features. Prints, checks and stripes require a very simple style with few pattern pieces. Rely on the fabric to be the dominant feature and avoid the clutter of a fussy design.

Right side of fabric

It is not always easy to distinguish the right or 'face' side of a fabric. Some fabrics, such as poplins, chambrays and other plain woven fabrics are similar on both sides.

The general rule is that the right side of the fabric is in the inside of the fabric roll to protect it. The better finish of the selvedge edge also indicates the face side.

Grain

Most woven fabrics have a certain amount of elasticity or stretch which varies according to the direction of the pull. The warp or lengthways grain runs the length of the fabric with the selvedge and has the least amount of stretch. The weft or crossways grain which runs across the fabric from selvedge to selvedge has more stretch. True bias or diagonal grain has the greatest stretch or elasticity and is cut at a 45 degree angle to both the warp and weft threads.

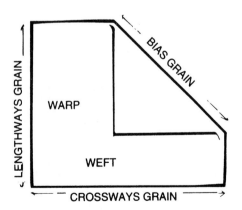

Cutting the garment on the correct grain is important to the fall or drape of the garment. Most pattern pieces are cut on the warp or lengthways grain.

Gathering or 'shirring' falls more softly and the fullness hangs more evenly when the gathering thread is run along the weft or crossways grain. The exception to this is when a slub or corded fabric is used and the cord is woven from selvedge to selvedge. Then it is better to gather or pleat the fabric along the weft or cross grain.

When in doubt regarding the best grain on which to gather fabric, test the fabric by running two rows of gathering stitches along the warp or lengthways grain and two rows on the weft or crossways grain. Draw up the gathering threads then choose the grain which gives the most pleasing results.

Straightening fabric

Always straighten the end of the fabric before cutting. The fabric can be cut, then torn across from selvedge to selvedge. If the fabric is not suitable for tearing, draw a weft thread out of the fabric from selvedge to selvedge. Cut along the drawn thread and the thread should be at right angles to the selvedge. If the weft thread is at a steep angle due to bad finishing after weaving, then the fabric must be straightened. To straighten, hold the fabric at each selvedge diagonally opposite each other and gently pull the shorter side, gradually working up the fabric. Check the angle of the grain until it is at right angles to the selvedge. If the angle is too steep to manage this method then wash the fabric to remove some of the finishing so that the material reverts to its original loomstate.

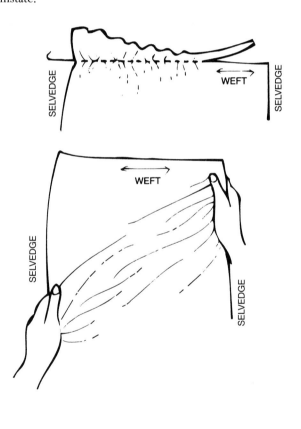

Shrinking fabric

Many woven cotton fabrics should be shrunk before use and this must be done before cutting. To shrink test washing fabrics, measure a 10cm (4") square of fabric and soak in water. Lightly press when almost dry, then measure. Pre-shrink all fabric if the measurements of the test piece have changed. Washable fabrics which are not pre-shrunk are best left in the original fold and soaked in water. When the water has penetrated every fibre, gently squeeze out the surplus, taking care not to wring the fabric. Keeping it still in folds, hang the fabric out to dry. Press before using.

Cutting

Nap or pile fabrics

Nap or pile fabrics must be cut one way only to prevent a mix of light and dark shading in the finished garment. To establish the direction of the nap, run your hand lightly over the surface of the fabric. The nap or pile is smoother running down and is lighter in appearance. When the pile is facing up, it is rougher to the touch and darker in appearance.

The general rule for this type of fabric is to cut velour, wool and similar fabrics with the nap running down.

Place the nap up for a darker appearance when cutting velvet, velveteen, corduroy or satin fabrics.

One-way designs are also cut to nap layout.

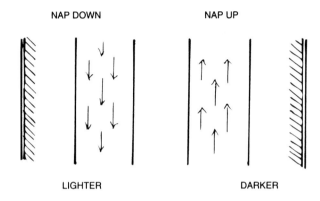

NAP DOWN	NAP UP
LIGHTER	DARKER

Patterned or printed fabric

Most plain and solid fabrics and those all-over prints without a definite one-way design can have the patterns dovetailed together in a fabric layout to save fabric (see page 13 for layout).

When the design is one-way, then the patterns have to be cut with all the pattern pieces facing one direction only. An example is a one-way floral print that must be cut this way to allow all flowers to stand upright with the stems down.

RIGHT WAY   WRONG WAY

Large patterned fabrics

Fabrics with very large or isolated motifs require the motifs to be positioned in the centre of each main pattern piece. This will give an all-over effect and prevent a bald appearance to sections of the garment.

This type of design requires more material which must be allowed for when buying the fabric.

The styling for these fabrics should be simple and with as few darts and seam lines as possible. To avoid a cluttered look to the finished garment, keep the front and back of the bodice in one piece.

RIGHT WAY   WRONG WAY

Checks and stripes

Carefully check all plaid, check, tartan and striped fabrics to see if they are the same on both sides of the main design line. If uneven, then they must be treated and cut as a one-way fabric. See page 13 for layout.

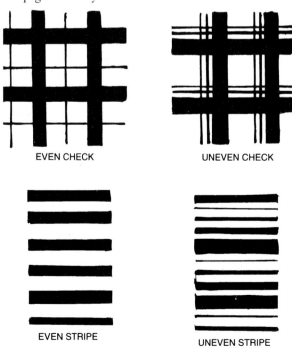

EVEN CHECK	UNEVEN CHECK
EVEN STRIPE	UNEVEN STRIPE

Garment fullness

Gathers and frills

The fabric grain must be considered when allowing for gathers and frills. Generally the fabric is cut from selvedge to selvedge to give a softer effect. If using a fine or sheer fabric, it is advisable to cut the fabric parallel to the selvedge to achieve a stiffer appearance to the gathers or frills. If the fabric is cut on the bias or diagonal, then more gathers must be allowed due to flattening of fullness.

To gauge the amount of fabric required, run two rows of gathering stitches along 40cm (16") of fabric from selvedge to selvedge and draw this up until the desired fullness is obtained. Frilling can be cut in various ways depending on the type of fabric used. The hem of the frill can be hand-rolled, slip stitched, machine hemmed, zig-zagged or picot edge finished.

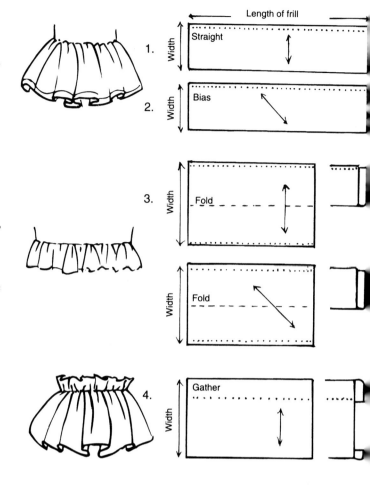

1. Single width, straight grain frills are best cut from crisp, finished fabric. The frills are cut the width of the frill plus the seam and hem allowance.

2. Bias-cut frills of single width are cut the same way as above and must have more fullness to look effective.

3. Straight grain or bias-cut frills of double width are the most suitable for fine and sheer fabric. The material is cut the width of the frill plus seam allowance, then multiplied by two.

4. Double edge frills are cut the width of both frills plus the top and lower hem allowance.

Tucks and pleats

The easiest method of preparing patterns for pleated or tucked garments is first to decide on the depth of the pleat and the distance between each one. Pleat the pattern paper, then lay the basic pattern in position and mark around the pattern.

It is easier for couture and home dressmakers to sew the pleats or tucks in a rectangle of fabric, allowing sufficient fabric for the depth of each pleat or tuck and the distance between. Press the fabric well before laying the pattern in position on the fabric, mark around and cut out.

This method can be used for permanently pleated fabric.

Pleating is another method of arranging fullness and is less bulky than gathers. The finished pleat can be left unpressed for a softer effect, be pressed flat or stitched down on each fold. Choose the most appropriate method for the design and the fabric.

Select a crease-resistant fabric which is capable of taking and holding a sharp crease under pressing. Before purchasing fabric, check that it is suitable for pleating.

All commercial paper patterns which include pleats have the pleating lines marked with arrows to indicate the direction they face. Paper patterns should be purchased by the hip measurement because it is comparatively simple to adjust the waist to fit if required.

It is advisable to shorten a pleated skirt from the waistline to avoid alterations to the hemline.

Knife pleats

The folds of the pleats face one direction only, from right to left. Allow a pleat to cover a front or a side seam placket or zipper.

To gauge the amount of fabric required allow approximately 3 times the measurement to be pleated by the length of the pleating.

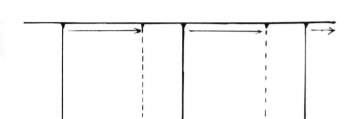

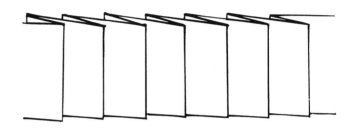

Box pleats

The fold edges of the pleats face each other with the folds meeting at the centre on the wrong side of the fabric.

To gauge the amount of fabric required allow approximately 3 times the measurement to be pleated by the length of the pleating.

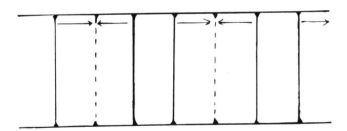

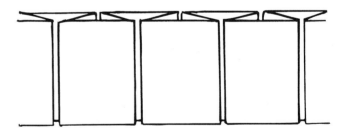

Inverted pleats

The two fold lines meet at the centre. This forms half a box pleat.

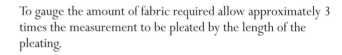

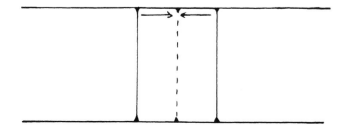

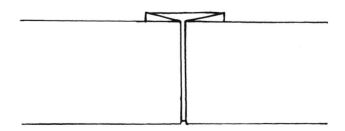

Patternmaking

The position given on the patterns for design lines, yokes, darts and seams can vary to suit individual tastes. The design line measurements given in this book are approximate. Each pattern piece must be marked with relevant information and notice must be taken at all times of these signs for the pattern and garment to be successful.

2. Heavy lines indicate pattern outline

   Thin lines indicate design lines

   Dot and dash lines indicate guide lines

   The sign of a graded square ruler indicates

   a definite right angle

   This sign indicates gathering stitching between

   balance marks

3. This sign indicates balance marks which correspond to those on another piece of pattern. This assists with the correct assembly of the garment. The general rule is that, for example, one balance mark on the front bodice armhole corresponds with the one on the front head of the sleeve pattern. There are two balance marks together on the back bodice armhole to correspond with the two on the back sleeve pattern.

4. The arrow between balance marks indicates the direction which a pleat or tuck must face. One balance mark is placed over the other to form a pleat.

5. 'Cut and spread' indicates to cut through the pattern from A to B and spread the amount required, be it by even or uneven amounts.

6. The term 'slash' means to cut the pattern to a given point to enable it to be 'spread' or opened out for fullness. The fullness required when 'slashing and spreading' a pattern is left to the discretion of the designer/patternmaker. Generally a soft, thin and pliable fabric is used for designs which require fullness in gathers, pleats or tucks as firm fabrics tends to stand out stiffly from the figure.

   The grain, weave or knit of the fabric must be carefully studied as most fabrics have a certain amount of elasticity or stretch in their construction which varies according to the direction of pull. In woven fabrics, the warp or lengthways grain has the least amount of stretch.

7. 'Slash and spread' indicates cutting the fabric from one point to another without severing the pieces before it is spread to the required amount.

   Often, when a pattern has been slashed and spread it alters the shape of the line and has to be reshaped for a smooth curve.

8. To 'pivot' or swing out a pattern piece gains additional fullness while retaining the shape of the pattern.

1. The grain line indicates the direction of the fabric grain on the pattern. This must be placed parallel to the selvedge of the fabric and is essential to the correct 'fall' of the garment. The grain line must be clearly marked on each pattern piece.

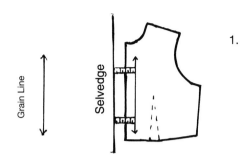

1.

3.

Front   Sleeve   Back

4.

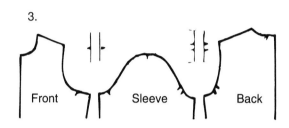

5.

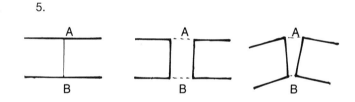

A   B   A   B   A   B

6.

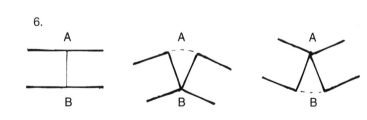

A   B   A   B   A   B

7.   8.

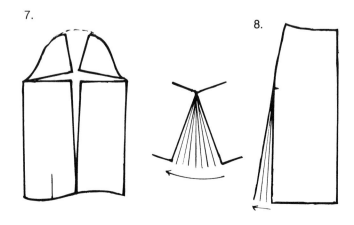

Darts

1. Darts have to be 'folded out' of a pattern before the seam allowance is added.

2. The dart is folded out of the pattern paper in the direction it will be pressed after sewing. The base of the dart is cut level with the seamline.

3. The dart is opened out and then the seam allowance is added to the complete pattern.

4. If the dart is very large or a sheer or knitted fabric is used, cut out the dart and add the seam allowance to the dart edge.

5. Avoid bulk over a darted neck edge by taking out the dart from the facing pattern.

6. Frequently a pattern is separated by slashing though the end of a dart. Round off this point to give the pattern a smoother sewing line.

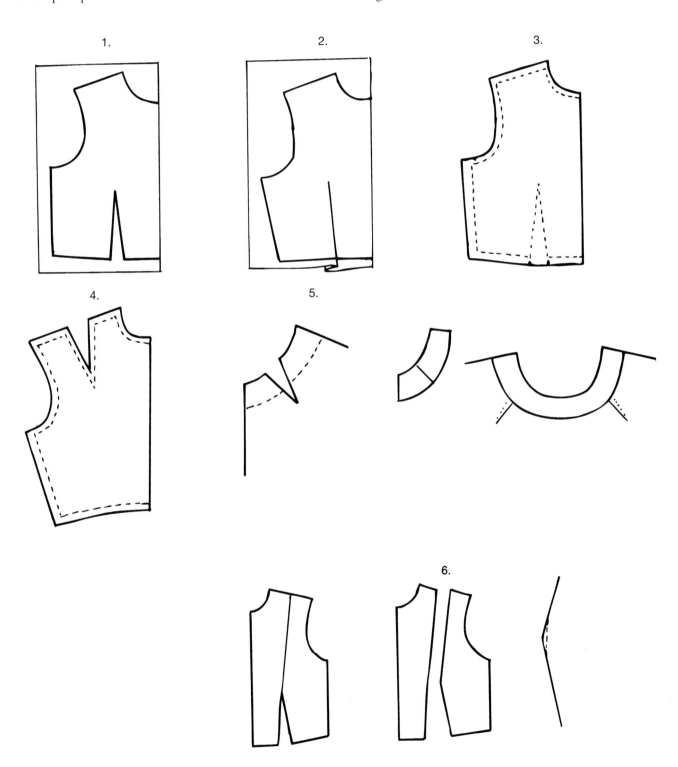

Seam allowance

When the pattern has been completed, a seam allowance must be added to all sewing edges. This amount varies depending on the type of fabric and the method of production.

In manufacturing, the seam allowance is governed by the machines used. Overlocker and dual needle machines have a predetermined 'bite' and the seam allowance on the pattern is marked accordingly.

In couture and home dressmaking, the seam allowance varies depending on the fabric used. A wider seam allowance is needed on tweeds to prevent fraying, while a narrower seam is required for fine and sheer fabrics and lightweight knits.

The seam allowance should not be less than the following as too much time and fabric can be wasted by cutting away any superfluous amount.

0.5cm (1/4") around the neck edge, collars, pocket flaps and facings.

1cm (3/8") at armholes, sleeve heads and around pockets.

1.5cm (5/8") at waist, side and shoulder seams and at the centre front and back seams.

Hem allowance will vary depending on the type of hem. The straighter the hemline, the wider the hem can be: 2cm (3/4") to 7cm (23/4") is general. The more shaped the hemline, the narrower the hem allowance has to be for easy turning, with 1cm (3/8") to 3cm (11/8") the usual width. A 1cm (3/8") width hem is all that is required for a hand rolled hem.

1.5cm (5/8") seam allowance is used on commercial paper patterns for all seams. The exception is for hems which will vary in width.

Check the pattern before use to ensure that all the grain lines are marked and corresponding balance marks or notches are in place.

A time saving method adopted by manufacturers is to add the seam allowance to the basic block patterns prior to use and then to add it on to any newly cut edges.

Throughout this book after the pattern is completed there is a reminder to add the seam allowance and to mark corresponding balance marks and the grain line on each pattern piece.

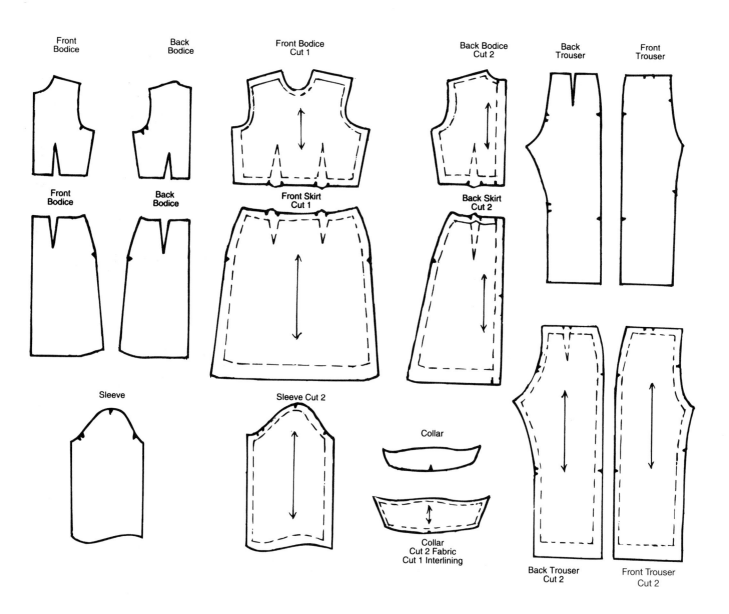

Pattern preparation

Always place the right sides of the fabric together, with the pattern pieces on top of the wrong side of the fabric.
Spread the fabric out on a long, flat table. If one is not available, then lay the fabric on the floor. Take care that the selvedge and warp threads lie absolutely straight.

The weft threads should fall at right angles to the selvedge when the fabric is folded on the lengthways grain. It is essential that the fabric lies correctly before cutting otherwise the garment will hang badly. This mistake cannot be rectified after making up.

1.

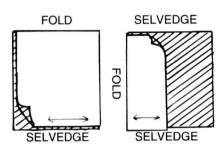

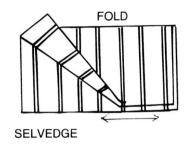

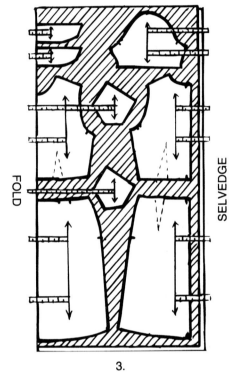

1. Take particular care when placing the pattern pieces on the fold of the fabric. Place the right sides of the fabric together and fold either with the selvedges together or on the weft crossways grain as required.
   Match any check or stripe fabric by placing one above the other, ensuring that the fold is parallel or at right angles to the selvedge of the fabric.

2. Arrange the pattern pieces on the correct grain lines and check with a tape measure or ruler that all grain lines run parallel to the selvedge.
   Check the layout and ensure that pattern pieces to be paired are laid the correct way to avoid cutting two right sleeves and no left sleeve.
   Before cutting out the pattern, always check that the correct number of pattern pieces have been laid in position.
   Pin a commercial printed paper to the fabric. When using a pattern cut from heavy pattern paper or board or when cutting a fabric which will mark such as velvet, use weights to hold the pattern flat and in position before marking around each pattern piece with chalk. Remove the pattern and cut out in the usual way.
   Be careful to mark all darts, buttonholes, balance marks and pocket positions before removing the pattern.

3. The best method to match checks, plaids, tartan and horizontal stripes successfully is to draw a line on the bodices to the armhole side seam point.
   Draw a line on the skirt at right angles from the centre front and back to the hipline.
   Draw a line on the sleeve at right angles from the centre of the sleeve to the armhole-underarm seam.
   All the garment's pattern pieces must be placed on the same matching fabric line with the centre front and back line down the dominant check or stripe. Place the centre line of the sleeve, collars and front facing on this line.

3.

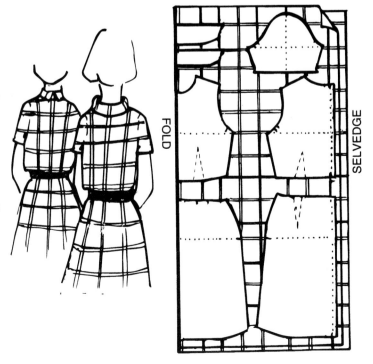

Basic bodice block draft

This basic front and back bodice draft is the block used as a foundation for all the pattern designs in this book. The front and back bodices are drafted together for convenience and can be separated at point H.

The front bodice is 2cm (3/4") wider than the back bodice to ensure that the side seams lie in the correct position. This corresponds to the waistline of the front and back skirt block draft.

8cm (31/8") ease has been allowed around the chest in this draft.
4cm (11/2") ease has been allowed around the waist in this draft.

Personal measurements can be substituted for those on the chart. For imperial version see p84.

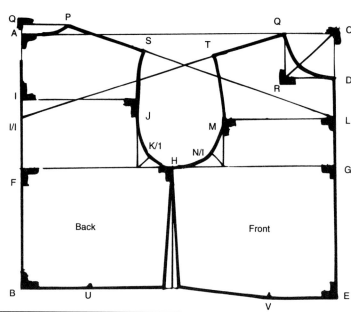

	Children			Girls & Boys				Centimetres
Size	2	4	6	8	10	12	14	
A-B	23.5	25.5	27.5	29.5	32	34.5	37	Centre back length. Square across from A and B.
A-C	32	34	36	38	40	42	44	Half chest measurement plus ease. Square down from C for centre front line.
C-D	4.8	5.2	5.6	6	6.4	6.8	7.2	Front neck depth. Square out from D.
D-E	19	21	23	25	27.5	30	32.5	Centre front line.
B-F	9	10.5	12	13.5	15	16.5	18	Side seam length. Square out from F to G on centre front line D-E.
F-H	15	16	17	18.5	19.5	20.5	21.5	Half back chest measurement plus ease and minus 1cm. Square down from H.
H-H/1	9	10.5	12	13.5	15	16.5	18	Equals B-F side seam length.
A-I	7.25	7.5	7.75	8	8.5	9	9.5	Half A-F.
I-J	11.5	12	12.5	14	14.75	15.5	16.25	Half across back measurement. Square down to K on line F-H.
K-K/1	2	2	2	2.5	2.5	2.7	2.7	Bisect angle J-K-H.
D-L	4.25	4.5	4.75	5	5.25	5.5	5.75	Half D-G.
L-M	11	11.5	12	13.5	14.25	15	15.75	Half across front measurement. Square down to N on line G-H.
N-N/1	1.5	1.5	1.5	2	2	2.5	2.5	Bisect angle M-N-H.
A-O	1.5	1.5	1.5	1.5	1.5	1.5	1.5	Back neck height. Square out from O.
O-P	4.6	5	5.4	5.8	6.2	6.6	7	
A-P								Join back with a curve.
C-Q	4.6	5	5.4	5.8	6.2	6.6	7	Equals O-P on back neck. Square down to R.
C-R								Join.
R-R/1	1.5	1.5	1.5	2.5	2.5	2.5	2.5	
D-Q								Join front neck shape with a curve.
I-I/1	2.5	2.5	2.5	2.5	2.5	2.5	2.5	
I-Q								Join for front shoulder slope.
L-P								Join for back shoulder slope.
P-S	7	7.5	8	9	9.5	10	10.5	Back shoulder length.
Q-T	7	7.5	8	9	9.5	10	10.5	Front shoulder length.
S-T								Join S-J-K/1-H-N/1-M-T for the armhole with a good curve.
B-U	6	6.5	7	7.5	8	8.5	9	Square out from B for back waistline.
E-V	6	6.5	7	7.5	8	8.5	9	Square out from E for front waistline.
H/1-W	1	1	1	1	1	1	1	
H/1-X	1	1	1	1	1	1	1	
H-W	9	10.5	12	13.5	15	16.5	18	Join.
H-X	9	10.5	12	13.5	15	16.5	18	Join.

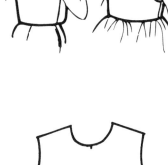

Front

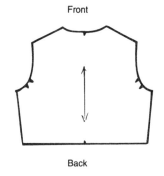

Back

On the front bodice armhole measure in 4cm from H for the position of the front sleeve balance mark.
On the back bodice armhole measure in 4cm and 5cm from H for the position of the back sleeve balance marks.
Separate the front and back bodices at H-Y and H-X.
This completes the basic front and back bodice block draft for children 2-4-6 and girls and boys 8-10-12-14.
The centre front and back can be placed on the fold or seam.
Add seam allowance and make corresponding balance marks.
Mark the grain line on each pattern piece.

Basic bodice block draft with darts

Proceed with the following construction for the front and back
waist darts for a more fitted waistline for girls' sizes 8-10-12-14.
For imperial version see p85.

				Girls				Centimetres
Size	2	4	6	8	10	12	14	
U-Y				11.5	12	12.5	13	Back dart length.
U-U/1				1	1.25	1.5	1.75	Half back dart width.
U-U/2				1	1.25	1.5	1.75	Half back dart width. Join U/1-Y-U/2 for back dart.
V-Z				13	13.5	14	14.5	Front dart length.
V-V/1				1	1.25	1.5	1.75	Half front dart width.
V-V/2				1	1.25	5	1.75	Half front dart width. Join V/1-Z-V/2 for front dart.

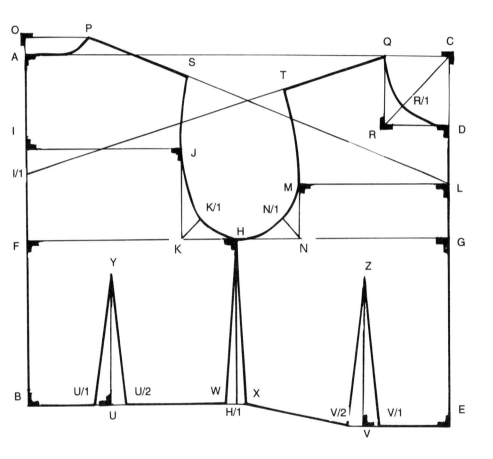

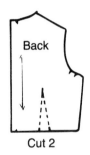

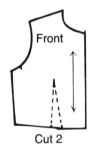

On the front bodice armhole measure 4cm in from H for the
position of the front sleeve balance mark.
On the back bodice armhole measure 4cm and 5cm in from H
for the position of the back sleeve balance marks.
This completes the basic front and back bodice block draft.
After separating the back bodice at H-W and front bodice at H-
X, place the shoulders together at the neck point to ensure that
there is a smooth curve to the neckline.
The centre front and back can be placed on the fold or the
seams.
Add seam allowance and make corresponding balance marks.
Mark the grain line on each pattern piece.

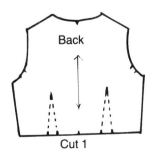

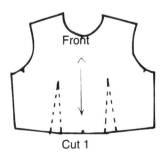

Bodice patterns

Use the basic front and back bodice block patterns as a foundation for the following.

Fitted front bodice

1. Mark C in the centre of the shoulder line A-B.
   Join C to D at the top of the dart.

2. Cut from C to D and separate the sections.
   Round D on the side bodice for a smoother line.

3. Add seam allowance and make corresponding balance marks.
   Mark the grain line on each pattern piece.

1.
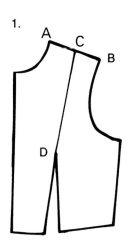

2.
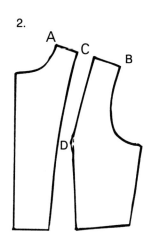

3.
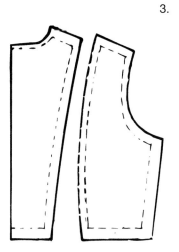

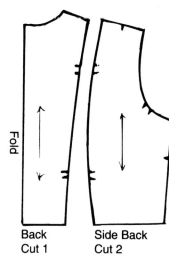

Back
Cut 1

Side Back
Cut 2

Fold

Fitted back bodice

1. Mark C in the centre of the shoulder line A-B.
   Join C to D at the top of the dart.

2. Cut from C to D and separate the sections.
   Round D on the side bodice for a smoother line.

3. Add seam allowance and make corresponding balance marks.
   Mark the grain line on each pattern piece.

1.
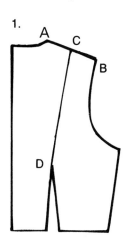

2.
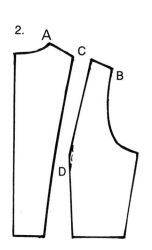

3.
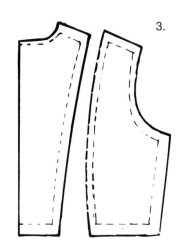

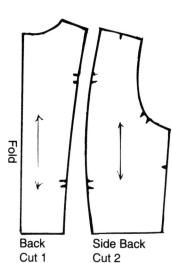

Back
Cut 1

Side Back
Cut 2

Fold

Use the basic front and back bodice block patterns as a
foundation for the following.

Shaped front bodice

1. Measure down approximately 5cm (2") from A to B on the
   armhole.
   Join B to C at the top of the dart.

2. Cut from B to C and separate the sections.
   Round C on the side bodice pattern for a smoother line.

3. Add seam allowance and make corresponding balance marks.
   Mark the grain line on each pattern piece.

1.

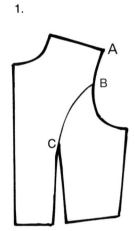

2.

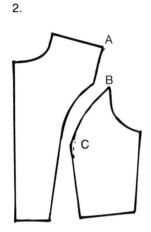

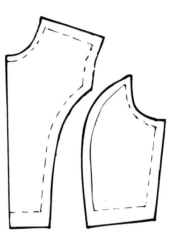

3.

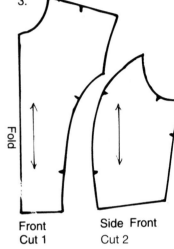

Front
Cut 1

Side Front
Cut 2

Shaped back bodice

1. Measure down approximately 9cm (31/2") from A to B on
   the armhole.
   Join B to C at the top of the dart.

2. Cut from B to C and separate the sections.
   Round C on the side bodice pattern for a smoother line.

3. Add seam allowance and make corresponding balance marks.
   Mark the grain line on each pattern piece.

1.

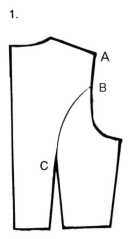

2.

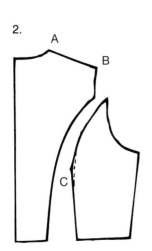

3.

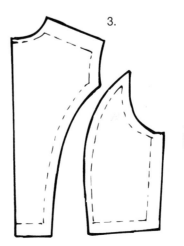

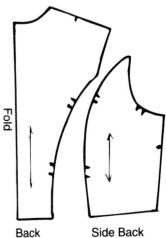

Back
Cut 1

Side Back
Cut 2

Use the basic front and back bodice pattern as a foundation for
the following.

Front bodice with shoulder yoke

1. Measure the depth of the shoulder yoke from A-B to C-D.
    Join E at the top of the dart to F on line C-D.

2. Cut through C-D and separate shoulder yoke.

3. Slash from F to E and close the waist dart.
   If greater fullness is required open the pattern more at F.
   Add seam allowance and make corresponding balance marks.
   Mark the grain line on each pattern piece.

1.

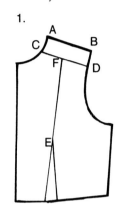

2.

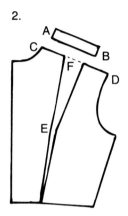

3.

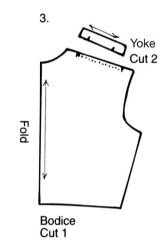

Back bodice with shoulder yoke

1. Measure the depth of the yoke required from C to D on the
    centre back line.
    Square across from D to E at the armhole.
    F is a quarter of line D-E marked from E.
    Square down from F to G on the waistline.

2. Cut through line D-E to separate the yoke.
    Cut through line F-G and spread to fullness required.
    Add seam allowance and make corresponding balance marks.
    Mark the grain line on each pattern piece.

1.

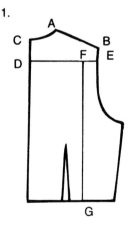

2.

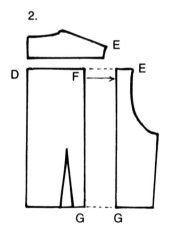

3.

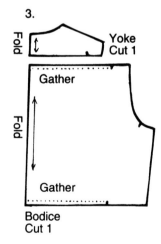

Back shirt yoke

The front and back yokes of a shirt are usually cut without a
shoulder seam.

1. Place the shoulder of the front and back yokes together at the
    neck edge A-B.

2. Add seam allowance and make corresponding balance marks.
    The centre back of the yoke can be placed on the fold or
    seamed. A shirt yoke is always cut double and 'bagged' out
    when sewing.
    Mark the grain line on each pattern piece.

1.

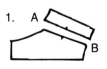

2.

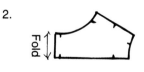

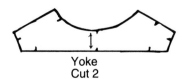

Use the basic front and back bodice patterns as a foundation for the following.

Front bodice with yoke and pleats

1. Measure the depth of the yoke required from A to B on the centre front line.
   Square across from B to C at the armhole.
   Draw a line up from D at the edge of the dart to E on B-C.
   Mark the pleat width from E to F. Square down to G at the waistline.

2. Cut through line B-C to separate yoke.
   Cut through lines E-D and F-G and spread for the pleat width.
   The dart allowance is added evenly into the under pleats.

3. Add seam allowance and make corresponding balance marks.
   Indicate the direction the pleats face on the pattern.
   Mark the grain line on each pattern piece.

1.

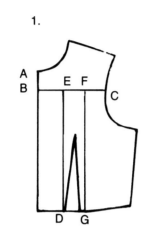

2.

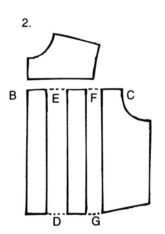

3.

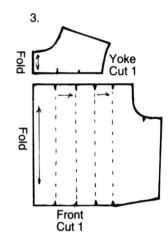

Back bodice with yoke and pleats

1. Measure the depth of the yoke required from A to B on the centre back line.
   Square across from B to C at the armhole.
   Draw up a line from E at the end of the dart to F on the yoke line and down to G at the waistline.
   H is the pleat width from F. Square down to J at the waistline.

2. Cut through B-C to separate the yoke.
   Cut through lines F-G and H-J and spread for the pleat width.
   The dart allowance is added evenly into the under pleats.

3. Add seam allowance and make corresponding balance marks.
   Indicate the direction on the pleats face on the pattern.
   Mark the grain line on each pattern piece.

1.

2.

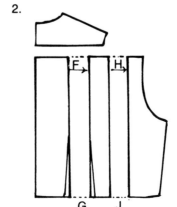

3.

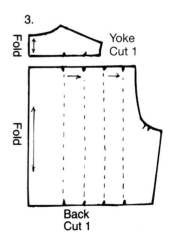

Use the basic front bodice block pattern as the foundation for the following.

Bodice with a rounded yoke

1. Mark down from A to C and from B to D the depth of the yoke required. Join C-D with a curve.
   Extend E at the top of the dart to F on the yoke line.
   Mark lines G-H and J-I parallel to the centre front.

2. Cut through line C-D to separate the yoke.
   Cut through line E-F and close the dart at the waistline.

Cut through lines G-H and J-I and spread evenly for the fullness required.

3. Place the centre front of the bodice and the yoke on the fold. Add seam allowance and make corresponding balance marks. Mark the grain line on each pattern piece.

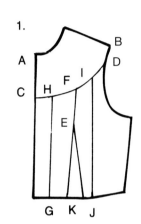

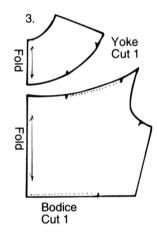

Bodice with a pointed yoke

1. Mark down from A to C and B to D for the shape of the yoke required.
   Join C to D.

2. Cut through line C-D to separate the yoke.

3. The yoke is placed on the fold and the centre front bodice is seamed. Ease the dart amount into the waistline.
   Add seam allowance and make corresponding balance marks. Mark the grain line on each pattern piece.

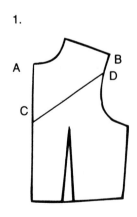

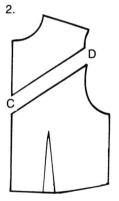

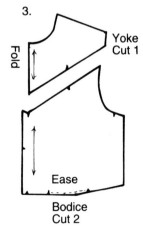

Use the basic front and back dress block and basic sleeve patterns as a foundation for the following.

Basic shirt and blouse pattern

Shirts and blouses require a looser fitting block pattern with a deeper armhole than the standard basic block drafts.

1. Place the centre front and back 2cm (3/4") apart with the chest A-B in line.
    Mark the shirt length required from C to D on the centre back line.
    Square across from D to E on the front and back side seams.
    From B lower the armhole by 0.5cm (1/4") and move out 1.25cm (1/2") to F.
    Reshape the armhole from G to F.
    Reshape the side seam from F to E with a parallel line.

2. On the sleeve pattern lower B 0.5cm (1/4") and move out 1.25cm (1/2") to C.
    From C draw a line parallel to the sleeve seam to E at the end of the sleeve.   Reshape sleeve head from C to A.
    Add seam allowances and make corresponding balance marks.
    Mark the grain line on each pattern piece.

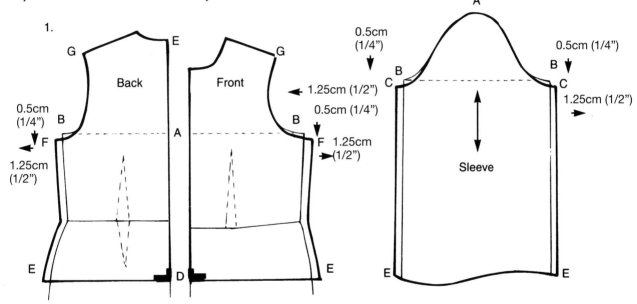

Sleeveless bodice

A sleeveless bodice or dress requires a slight alteration to the pattern to prevent gaping at the armholes.

1. Mark in 1cm (3/8") from A to B on the shoulder line.
    Mark in 1cm (3/8") and up 1cm (3/8") from C to D at the armhole/side seam point.

Reshape the armhole from B to D.
Reshape the side seam by joining D to E at the waistline.

2. Add seam allowance and make corresponding balance marks.
    Mark the grain line on each pattern piece.

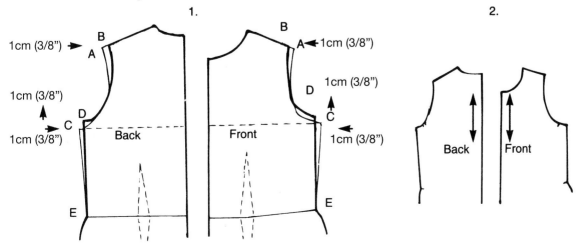

Bodice fastening

Buttons and buttonholes

Use the basic front and back bodice patterns as a foundation for the following.

Buttons and buttonholes can be added to any type of garments. The width of the fastening wrap for buttoning is determined by the size of the button and the direction of the buttonhole. A wider wrap is necessary for a larger size coat button, while a narrower one is often used on babywear. The wrap must extend 1cm (3/8") beyond the edge of the button.

It is necessary to reinforce behind the button and buttonhole with a suitable interfacing fabric to prevent strain at these stress points.

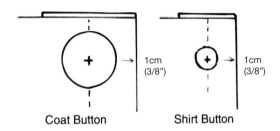

Coat Button   Shirt Button

Girls' buttoning

The buttons are always placed on the left side of girls' garments with the buttonhole on the right side. This rule applies whether the garment is buttoned at the centre front or back.

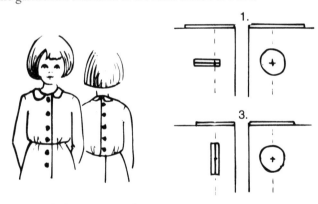

Boys' buttoning

The buttons are always placed on the right side of a boys' garment with the buttonhole on the left side. This rule applies whether the garment is buttoned at the centre front or back.

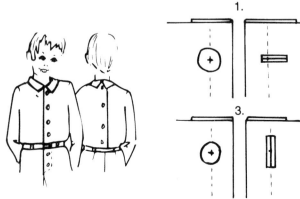

Position of buttons and buttonholes

Fastening for girls and boys are on opposite sides. Although girls do not mind wearing boys' shirts wrapping towards the right side, no boy would ever wear a shirt wrapping the girls' way to the left.

Take care to check the correct fastening side before marking and making buttonholes on any garment.

1. Horizontal buttonholes are placed to extend 0.5cm (1/4") beyond the centre front and back lines to allow for the 'stalk' of the button's thread which is placed on the centre line.

2. This diagram shows the correct position of the buttonhole in relation to the button.

3. Vertical buttonholes are placed on the centre front or back line.

4. This diagram shows the correct position of a vertical buttonhole in relation to the button.

5. These diagrams show the correct position of buttons and buttonholes on the front and back bodices.

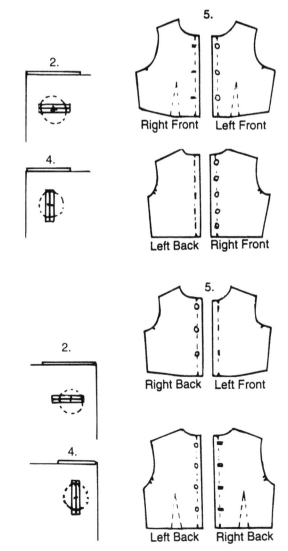

Front fastening facing

The measurements given for the wraps below are approximate and are based on a standard size shirt button.

1. For the front wrap mark C-D 2cm (3/4") from the centre line A-B.
   For the front facing pattern mark F 4cm (11/2") from E at the neck point on the shoulder and G 4cm (11/2") from B at the waistline.
   Join F-G with a curve.

2. Mark a separate pattern for the facing by tracing C-E-F-G-D-C.

3. The front facing can be cut in one with the front bodice by placing line C-D on the fold of the pattern paper and tracing off the facing.

4. Cut an interfacing pattern for the button and buttonhole support.
   Add seam allowance and make corresponding balance marks. Mark the position of button and buttonholes on the pattern.

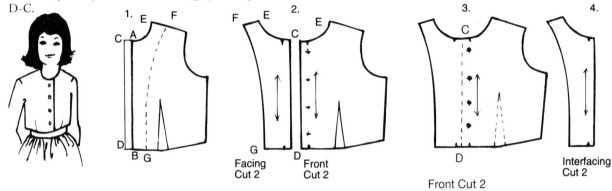

1.
Facing Cut 2

2.
Front Cut 2

3.
Front Cut 2

4.
Interfacing Cut 2

Back neck facing

Most neckline and collars require a back neck facing. The shoulder width must match that of the front neck facing.

1. Mark down 4cm (11/2") from A on centre back line to C.
   Mark 4cm (11/2") from D on the neck point to E on the shoulder line.
   Join C-E with a curve parallel to the back neck line.

2. Place the back neck facing on the fold.

3. Add seam allowance and make corresponding balance marks.

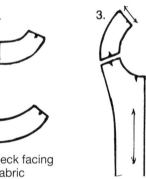

2.
Fold

Back neck facing
Cut 1 fabric
Cut 1 interfacing

Back fastening facing

1. For the back wrap mark C-D 2cm (3/4") from the centre front line A-B.
   For the back facing pattern mark F 4cm (11/2") from E at the neck point on the shoulder and G 4cm (11/2") from B at the waistline.
   Join F-G as illustrated.

2. Make a separate facing pattern by tracing C-E-F-G-D-C.

3. The back facing can be cut in one piece with the back bodice by placing line C-D on the fold of the pattern paper and tracing off the facing.

4. Cut an interfacing pattern for button and buttonhole support.
   Add seam allowance and make corresponding balance marks. Mark the position of button and buttonholes on the pattern.

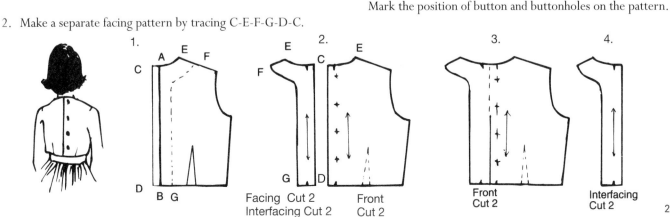

1.

2.
Facing Cut 2
Interfacing Cut 2

Front
Cut 2

3.
Front
Cut 2

4.
Interfacing
Cut 2

23

Shirt front buttoning

This style is ideal for vertical buttonholes. Reverse the patterns for girls' fastening and use the front bodice patterns.

1. For the front band mark 2cm (3/4") out from the centre front line A-B for C-D and E-F.

2. Make the front band by tracing C-D-F-E-C.
   Add seam allowance and make corresponding balance marks.
   Mark the position of the buttons and buttonholes on the pattern.

3. This pattern has a full front facing which can be worn open to form revers or lapels.
   Mark 2cm (3/4") out from centre front line A-B for C-D and E-F.
   Mark G 4cm (11/2") from B and I 4cm (11/2") from H. Join G to I.

4. For the band and facing, place line C-D on the fold and trace off H-I-G.
   The front of the bodice pattern is now on line E-F.
   Trace off interfacing pattern C-D-G-I-H-C.
   Add seam allowance and make corresponding balance marks.
   Mark the position of button and buttonholes on the pattern.

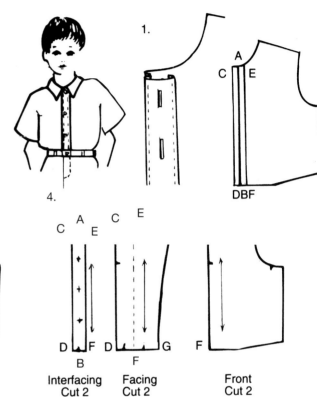

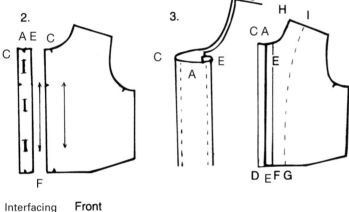

2.

Interfacing
Cut 2

Front
Cut 2

3.

4.

Interfacing
Cut 2

Facing
Cut 2

Front
Cut 2

DBF

Double breasted buttoning

This style is suitable for larger sizes. Suggested wrap width is 10cm (41/4") for sizes 8 and 10 and 14cm (51/2") for sizes 12 and 14.
Care must be taken in selecting the correct size button.
Generally the buttonholes are only on the edge of the wrap. The other buttons are stitched onto the front of the garment.
Use the front bodice or coat pattern as a foundation for the following.
Reverse the pattern for boys' fastenings.

1. Mark out half the wrap width from A-B at centre front; that is approximately 5cm (2") for sizes 8 and 10 and 7cm (23/4") for sizes 12 and 14.
   Mark G from B and I from H for front facing. Join G to I with a curve.
   Make the facing wide enough to take the buttons and buttonholes.

2. Make a separate facing and interfacing by tracing off C-H-I-G-D-C
   Add seam allowance and make corresponding balance marks.
   Mark the grain line on each pattern piece.

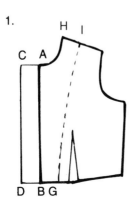

1.

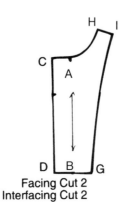

D B G

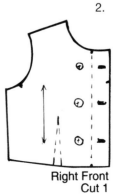

Facing Cut 2
Interfacing Cut 2

2.

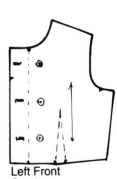

Right Front
Cut 1

Left Front
Cut 1

Neckline patterns

Use the basic front and back patterns as a foundation for the following.

High round neckline

1. Place the front and back shoulders together at A-B.
   Mark down 4cm (11/2") from C to D at the centre front and E to F at the centre back for the facing width at D-H-F.
   Join D to F marking the facing parallel to the neckline C-A-E.

2. Place the centre front bodice and the facing C-D on the fold.
   Add seam allowance and make corresponding balance marks.
   Mark the grain line on each pattern piece.

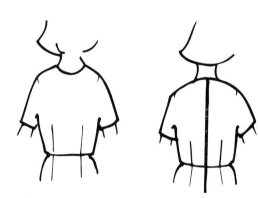

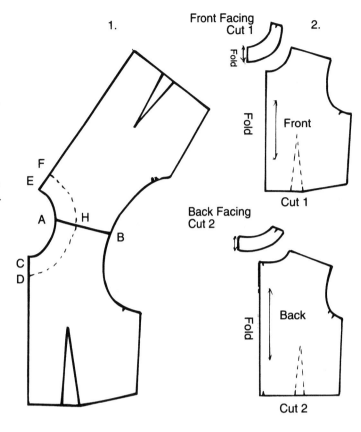

Scoop neckline

This neckline can be cut away from the neck.

1. Place the front and back shoulders together at A-B.
   Mark the desired depth of neckline down from C to D at the front and from E to F at the back. Join D to F for new neckline.
   Mark the neck facing 4cm (11/2") wide and parallel to the neckline D-G-F for the facing width at J-H-K.

2. Place the centre front and back bodices on the fold.
   Place the centre front facing D-J and the back facing F-K on the fold.
   Add seam allowance and make corresponding balance marks.
   Mark the grain line on each pattern piece.

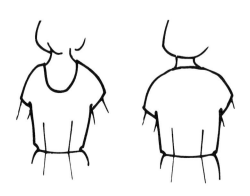

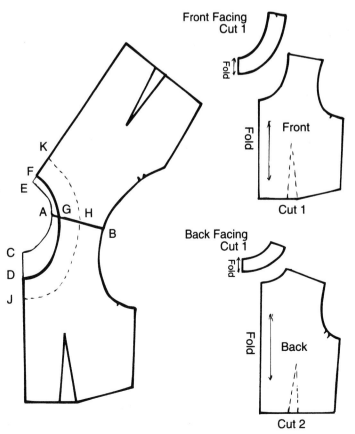

Use the basic front and back bodice patterns as a foundation for the following.

Vee neckline

1. Place the front and back shoulder together at A-B.
   Mark the depth of the front neckline from C to D and join to A.
   Mark the neck facing 4cm (11/2") wide and parallel to the neckline D-A-E.
   Round the facing at H for ease when sewing.

2. Place the centre front and back bodices on the fold.
   Place the front facing D-J and the back facing F-K on the fold.
   Add seam allowance and make corresponding balance marks.
   Mark the grain line on each pattern piece.

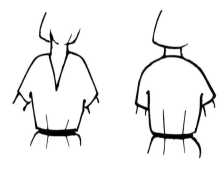

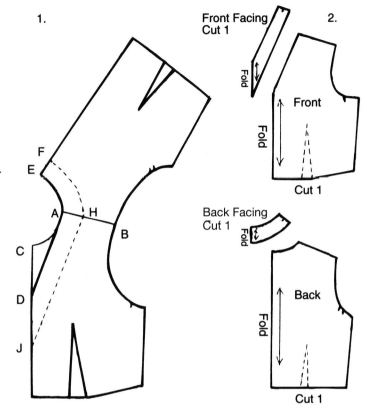

Wide vee neckline

1. Place the front and back shoulder together at A-B.
   Mark the depth of the neckline down from C to D at the front and E to F at the back.
   Mark from A to G the distance of the neckline required.
   Join D to G to F.
   Mark the neck facing 4cm (11/2") wide and parallel to the neckline D-G-F.
   Round the facing at H for ease when sewing.

2. Place the front facing D-J and the back facing F-K on the fold.
   Add seam allowance and make corresponding balance marks.
   Mark the grain line on each pattern piece.

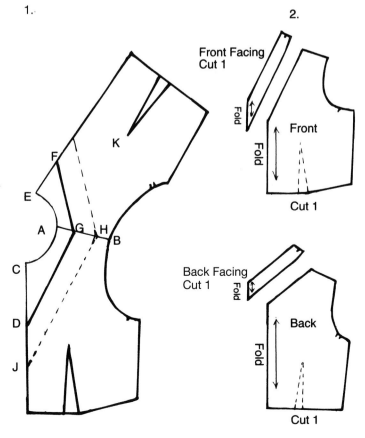

Use the basic front and back bodice patterns as a foundation for the following.

Wide square neckline

1. Place the front and back shoulders together at A and B.
   Mark the depth of the front neckline down from C to D and on the back bodice mark down from E to F.
   Square out from D to G across half the front neckline.
   Square out from F to H. Join G to H.
   Mark the neck facing 4cm (11/2") wide and parallel to the neckline D-G-H-F. Round corners at L and M.

2. Place the centre front and back bodices on the fold.
   Place the centre front facing D-J and the centre back facing F-K on the fold.
   Add seam allowance and make corresponding balance marks.
   Mark the grain line on each pattern piece.

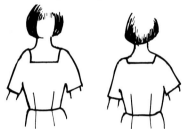

1.

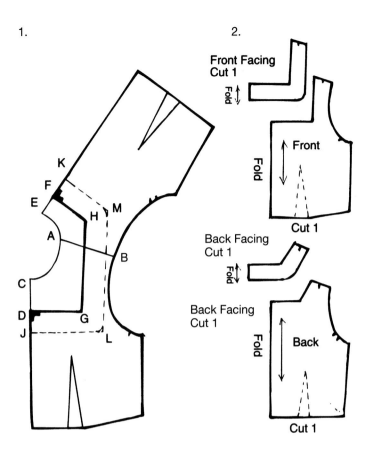

2.

Sleeveless bodice with a square neckline

The neck and armhole facings on a sleeveless bodice can be combined to prevent bulk on the shoulders.

Use the basic sleeveless front and back bodices as a foundation for the following.

1. Mark the front and back neckline as in the wide square neckline pattern above.
   For the facing, mark down 4cm (11/2") from D to J and from F to K.
   Square out from J to L and K to M.
   Mark down 4cm (11/2") from N to O and P to R at the side seams.
   Join O to L and R to M, making the facing parallel to the armhole.
   Curve the facing at L and M for ease when sewing.

2. Place the centre front and back bodices on the fold.
   Place the centre front facing D-J and the centre back facing F-K on the fold.
   Add seam allowances and make corresponding balance marks.

1.

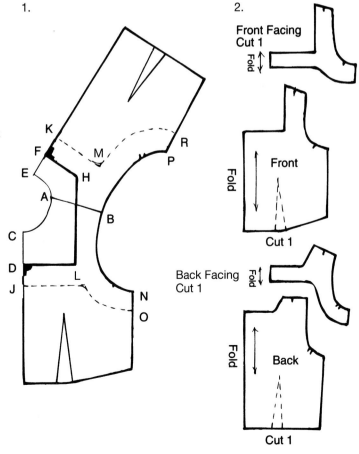

2.

Collar patterns

The closer the neck edge is to the bodice neck shape, the flatter the collar will lie on the shoulders.

Peter Pan and sailor collars are flat collars while mandarin and shirt collars stand high against the neck.

Use the front and back bodice patterns as a foundation for the following.

These collar styles lie flat on the shoulder with a slight roll at the neck line which covers the neck seam.

Peter Pan collar

1. Place the front and back bodices together at A at the neck point and overlap the shoulder at B by 1cm (3/8") for sizes 2-4-6 and 1.5cm (5/8") for sizes 8-10-12-14.
   Trace around the neck edge of the front and back bodices. Mark the collar width at approximately half the shoulder length from C to E at the centre back neck. Mark an equal amount around the neck edge and the curve to D at the centre front neck.

2. Place the centre back line C-E on the fold.

3. Add seam allowance and make corresponding balance marks. Mark the grain line on each pattern piece.
   A is at the shoulder seam point.

Two-piece Peter Pan collar

1. This collar is constructed in the same way as the basic Peter Pan collar except that it is rounded at E on the centre back.

2. Add seam allowance and make corresponding balance marks. Mark the grain line on each pattern piece.

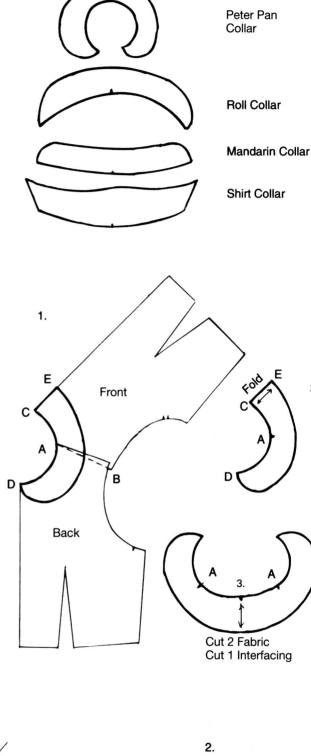

Peter Pan Collar

Roll Collar

Mandarin Collar

Shirt Collar

Cut 2 Fabric
Cut 1 Interfacing

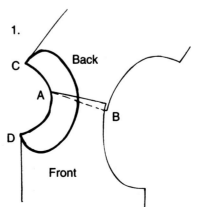

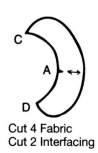

Cut 4 Fabric
Cut 2 Interfacing

Use the basic front and back bodice block patterns as a
foundation for the following.

Flat collars

These collars are constructed in the same way as the Peter Pan
collar. The only difference is in the shaping from D at the centre
front to line C-F at the centre back.

1. Place the front and back bodice together at A at the neck
   point and overlap the shoulders at B by 1cm (3/8") for sizes
   2-4-6 and 1.5cm (5/8") for sizes 8-10- 12-14.
   Trace around the neck edge for the front and back bodices.
   Mark the collar shape and width required from D to C.

2. Place centre back line C-F or C-E on the fold. Both are
   centre back seams, while C-G is cut away and has a seam.
   Add seam allowance and make corresponding balance marks.
   Mark the grain line on each pattern piece.
   A is at the shoulder seam point.

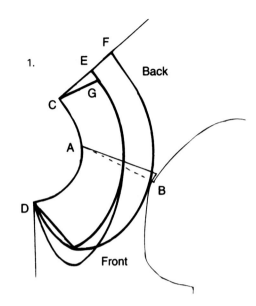

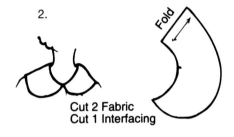

Cut 2 Fabric
Cut 1 Interfacing

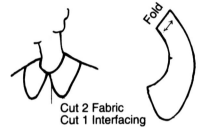

Cut 2 Fabric
Cut 1 Interfacing

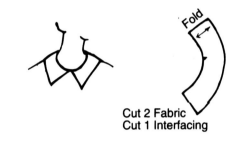

Cut 2 Fabric
Cut 1 Interfacing

Swallow collar

1. Place the front and back bodices together at A at the neck
   point and overlap the shoulders at B by 1cm (3/8") for sizes
   2-4-6 and 1.5cm (5/8") for sizes 8-10-12-14.
   Trace around the bodice patterns.
   Mark down from C to D for the depth of the neckline
   required.
   Mark the depth of the back collar from E to F on the centre
   back line.
   Shape from D to F.

2. Place centre back line E-F on the fold.
   Add seam allowance and make corresponding balance marks.
   Mark the grain line on each pattern piece.
   A is at the shoulder seam point.

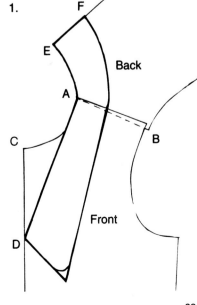

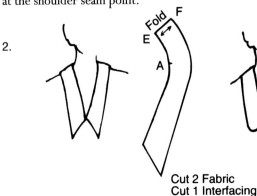

Cut 2 Fabric
Cut 1 Interfacing

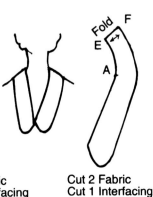

Cut 2 Fabric
Cut 1 Interfacing

29

1.

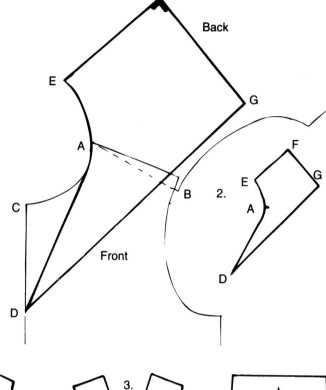

Use the basic front and back bodice patterns as a foundation for the following.

Sailor collar

1. Place the front and back bodices together at A at the neck point and overlap the shoulder at B by 1cm (3/8") for sizes 2-4-6 and 1.5cm (5/8") for sizes 8-10-12-14.
   Trace around the bodice neck patterns.
   Mark the depth of the neckline required down from C to D.
   Join A to D.
   Mark the depth of the back collars from E to F on the centre back line.
   Square from F to G and join to D.

2. The collar is D-A-E-F-G-D. A is the shoulder point.

3. Place centre back line E-F on the fold.
   Add seam allowance and make corresponding balance marks.
   Mark the grain line on each pattern piece.

  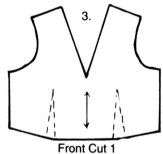

3.

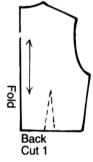 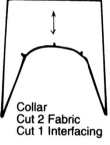

Back Cut 1

Front Cut 1

Collar
Cut 2 Fabric
Cut 1 Interfacing

Sailor collar with a dickie

1.

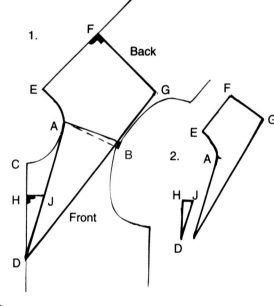

Back

A collar with a deep neckline often requires a front piece or a 'dickie' for modesty or to prevent the neckline gaping.
This collar is constructed in the same way as the sailor collar above.

1. To construct the dickie, mark the depth required down from C to H and square across to J on the bodice.

2. Trace off the collar D-A-E-F-G-D and the dickie J-H-D-J.

3. Place line E-F on the collar and D-H on the dickie on the fold. A is at the shoulder seam point.
   Add seam allowance and make corresponding balance marks.
   Mark the grain line on each pattern piece.

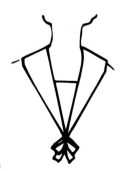 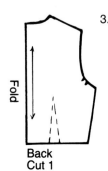

3.

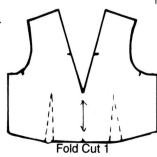 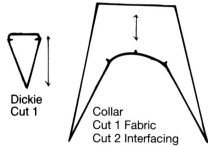

Back Cut 1

Fold Cut 1

Dickie Cut 1

Collar
Cut 1 Fabric
Cut 2 Interfacing

Mandarin collar

This is a high standing collar which fits close to the neck. Do not make this collar more than 4cm (11/2") wide or it will be too uncomfortable to wear.

1. Mark half the neck measurement from A to B.
   A-C is the collar width required.
   Square up from B across from C to D.
   A-E is half the back measurement and shoulder point.
   Divide B-E into 4 sections.

2. Slash each section from C-D to B-E.
   Overlap each section and raise B 1.5cm (5/8").
   Point D can be either square or rounded as required.

It is not necessary to draft elaborate patterns for the simple collars that follow below. All that is required is the neck measurement and the width of the collar.
These patterns can be cut double width and placed on the bias grain to give a softer roll edge to the collar.

3. Place A-C centre back on the fold.
   Add seam allowance and make corresponding balance marks.
   Mark the grain line on each pattern piece.

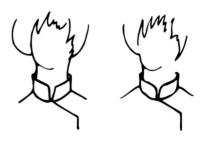

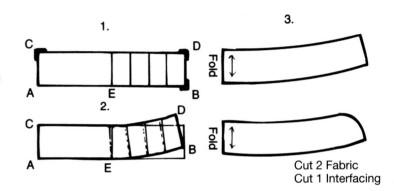

Cut 2 Fabric
Cut 1 Interfacing

Polo collar

1. Draw a rectangle of the neck measurement by twice the width of the collar.
   Add seam allowance and make corresponding balance marks.
   Mark the grain line on each pattern piece.

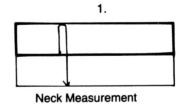
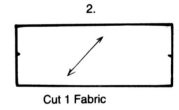

Neck Measurement   Cut 1 Fabric

Turtle collar

1. Draw a rectangle the neck measurement by four times the width of the collar.
   Add seam allowance and make corresponding balance marks.
   Mark the grain line on each pattern piece.
   This collar can be fastened several different ways at the centre back neck.
a) This collar is zip-fastened through the double thickness of the collar which will hold the collar high against the neck.

b) This collar is zip-fastened half way up the collar at the roll over which will give more ease around the neck.
c) This collar is stitched at the neckline only which will cause it to lie lower at the centre front and flatten the garment at the centre back neck.

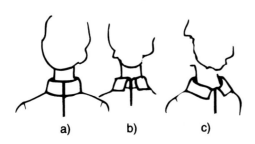

a)   b)   c)

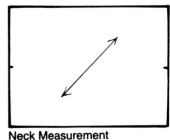

Four times the collar width

Cut 1 Fabric

Neck Measurement

Use the basic block or blouse patterns as the foundation for the following.

Roll collar

Trace around the front bodice neckline, then draft the collar.

1. Lower the front neck 1cm (3/8") down from A to B.
   Join B to C with a curve.
   Mark the half neck measurement from B through C to D.
   Square out from D 3cm (11/8") to E.

2. Square down from E to F on the shoulder line and curve to B.
   Mark approximately 7cm (23/4") for the width of the collar from E to G.
   Shape from B to H as required. Join H to G.

3. Trace off the collar. Add the fastening wrap out from B.
   Divide the collar into 3 equal sections.

4. Slash from line H-G to B-E and spread each section 0.5cm (1/4").

5. Place the centre back E-F on the fold.
   Add seam allowance and make corresponding balance marks.
   Mark the grain line on each pattern piece.

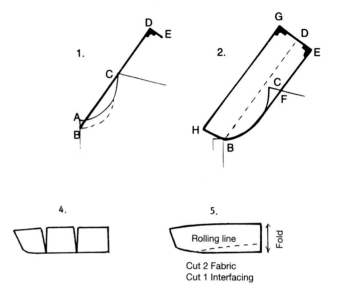

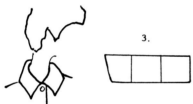

Basic blouse collar

This collar has a roll at the centre back and tends to flatten towards the centre front neck.

Trace around the front bodice neckline, then draft the collar.

1. Lower the front neck 1cm (3/8") from A to B.
   Reshape the neckline from B to C.
   Draw a line half the neck measurement from B through C to D.
   Pivot line C-D 2cm (3/4") to E for the back collar stand.
   Join E to C.

2. Square out from E approximately 6cm (23/8") to F for the width of the collar.
   Shape B-G-F as required.
   Trace off the collar pattern. Add the fastening wrap out from B.

3. Add seam allowance and make corresponding balancemarks.
   Mark the grain line on each pattern piece.
   Place the centre back line E-F on the fold.

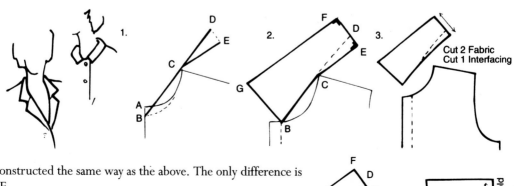

These collars are constructed the same way as the above. The only difference is shaping from B-G-F.

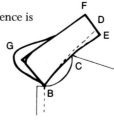

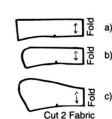

Use the basic front bodice or blouse block pattern as the foundation for the following.

Shirt collar with a stand

Trace around the neckline, then draft the collar with attached stand.

1. Draw a line from A to B.
    Square out 2.5cm (1") from A to C.
    Square out half the neck measurement from C to D.
    Square out 4cm (11/2") from D to E for the depth of the collar stand.

2. Square a line D-E to F on the shoulder line.
    Join F to A and extend 2cm (3/4") to G for the fastening wrap.
    Shape the wrap for the collar stand from C to G.

3. To draft the collar, trace off the collar stand A-G-C-D-E-F-A.
    Extend the centre back line D-E 1.5cm (5/8") to H.
    Shape as required approximately 6cm (23/8") from C to J and join to H.
    Trace off collar C-D-H-J-C and separate the stand A-G-C-D-E-A.

4. Place line C-D on the collar and stand together and trace around this pattern.
    Place centre back line D-H of the collar and D-E of the stand on the fold.

5. Add seam allowance and make corresponding balance marks. Mark the grain line on each pattern piece.

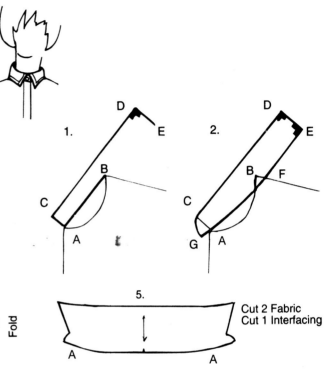

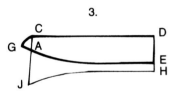

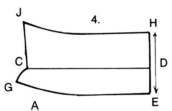

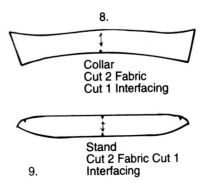

Shirt collar with separate stand

Draft this collar in the same way as above to stage 4.

6. Divide the collar line C-D into 3 equal sections.

7. Slash from line H-J to line C-D and spread each section 0.5cm (1/4") for a slight collar roll.

8. Add seam allowance and make corresponding balance marks. Mark the grain line on each pattern piece.

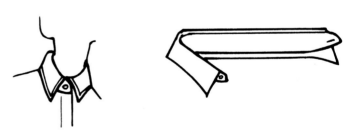

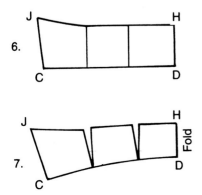

Basic sleeve block draft

This basic sleeve draft is the block pattern used as a foundation for all the sleeve pattern designs in this book.

An allowance has been added to the head of the sleeve so that it can be eased into the armhole of the front and back bodice block drafts.

Approximately 2cm (3/4") ease has been allowed for sizes 2-4-6 and 2.5cm (1") for sizes 8-10-12-14.

4cm (11/2") ease has been allowed around the biceps.

The underarm seam of this sleeve block draft is straight as children require loose fitting sleeves in their garments.

The back of the wrist hem is longer than the front to allow for the natural bend in the arm. It also gives a better balance to the sleeve.

Personal measurements can be substituted for those on the chart. For imperial version see p86.

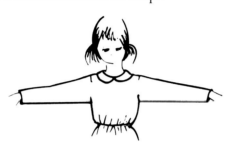

Sizes	Children			Girls & Boys				Centimetres
	2	4	6	8	10	12	14	
A-B	9	9.5	10	11	11.5	12	12.5	Sleeve crown height. Square across from A and B.
B-C	24	27	30	33	35	37	39	Underarm length. Square across from C.
A-D	22	23	24	26	27	28	29	Bicep measurement plus ease. Square down from D and E.
B-F								Square across to D-E.
A-G	11	11.5	12	13	13.5	14	14.5	Half A-D. Square down to H on line C-E.
A-I	3	3.2	3.4	3.6	3.8	4	4.2	Approximately 1/3 of line A-B. Square across to line D-F.
B-J	3	3.2	3.4	3.6	3.8	4	4.2	Approximately 1/3 of line A-B. Square across to line D-F.
I-K	6.8	7.1	7.4	7.8	8.1	8.4	8.7	
J-L	5	5.2	5.4	5.8	6.1	6.4	6.7	
K-M	9.5	10	10.5	11	11.5	12	12.5	
L-N	13.5	14	14.5	15	15.5	16	16.5	
B-F								Join B-L-K-G-M-N-F for sleeve head shape.
C-P	5.5	5.75	6	6.5	6.75	7	7.25	1/4 line C-E.
E-O	5.5	5.75	6	6.5	6.75	7	7.25	1/4 line C-E.
Q-O	0.5	0.5	0.5	1	1	1	1	Mark down for back wristline.
P-R	0.5	0.5	0.5	1	1	1	1	Mark up for front wristline.
C-E								Join C-R-H-Q-E for wristline.

For the front sleeve balance mark measure up 4cm from E on the front sleeve head.
For the back sleeve balance measure up 4cm and 5cm from F on the back sleeve head.
Add seam allowance and make corresponding balance marks.
Mark the grain line on each pattern piece.
The wrist edge of the sleeve can be finished with a hem, facing, binding, cuff or elasticised.

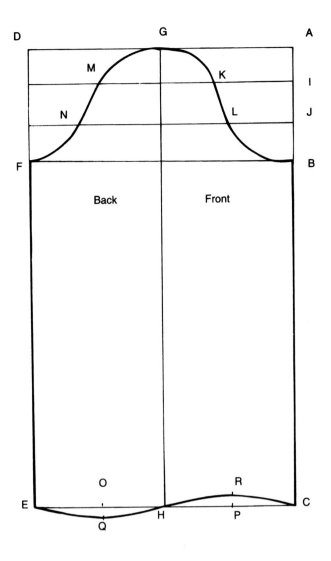

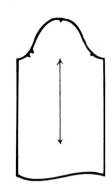

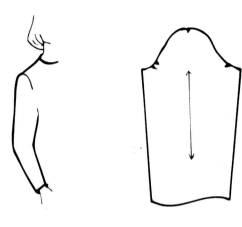

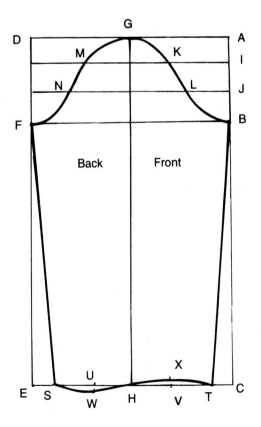

Tapered sleeve

Use the following draft for a sleeve more fitted at the wrist. This sleeve is more suitable for sizes 8-10-12-14. Check that the hand can be comfortably pulled through the reduced wristline. For imperial version see p87.

For imperial version see p87.

	Girls & Boys				Centimetres
Size	8	10	12	14	
E-S	2.5	2.5	2.5	2.5	
C-T	2.5	2.5	2.5	2.5	Equals E-S.
F-S					Join.
B-T					Join.
H-U	5.25	5.5	5.75	6	Half H-S.
H-V	5.25	5.5	5.75	6	Half H-T.
U-W	1	1	1	1	Mark down for back wristline.
V-X	1	1	1	1	Mark down for front wristline.
S-T					Join S-W-H-X-T for the wristline.

Add seam allowance and make corresponding balance marks.
Mark the grain line on each pattern piece.

Sleeve patterns

Basic short sleeve

Use the basic sleeve block pattern as a foundation for
the following.

	Children			Girls & Boys				
Size	2	4	6	8	10	12	14	
A-B	1 1/2	2	2 1/2	2 3/4	3	3 1/2	4 1/4	Approximate seam length (inches).
A-B	4	5	6	7	8	9	10	Approximate seam length (centimetres).

1. Mark down from A to B the sleeve length required.

2. Allow approximately 2.5cm (1") for the hem if cut in one
    with the sleeve.

3. The sleeve can be cut with a separate facing. Make this
    pattern approximately 2.5cm (1") wide.
    Add seam allowance and make corresponding balance marks.
    Mark grain line on all pattern pieces.

1.

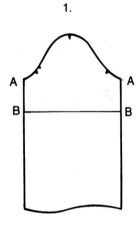

2.

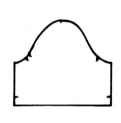

3.

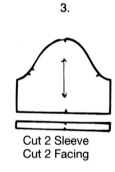

Cut 2 Sleeve
Cut 2 Facing

Tapered short sleeve with cuff

1. Mark down from A to B the length of the sleeve required.
    To taper the sleeve for a neater fit, mark in 1.5cm (5/8")
    from B to C. Join C to A.

2. To cut the cuff in one with the sleeve allow approximately
    3cm (11/8") for the cuff width and 3cm (11/8") for the
    turnover.

3. The cuff can be cut separately from the sleeve. Make the
    pattern as in diagram 2.
    Add seam allowance and mark corresponding balance marks.
    Mark the grain line on all pattern pieces.

1.

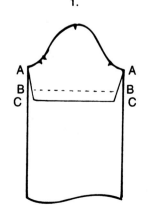

2.

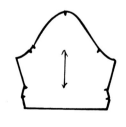
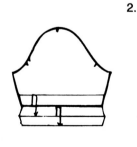

3.

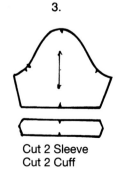

Cut 2 Sleeve
Cut 2 Cuff

Use the basic sleeve block pattern as a foundation for the following.

Cuffs

Cuffs add interest to a sleeve. These are more suitable for the larger sizes of 8-10-12-14.

A plain cuff without fastening must have a circumference large enough to pull comfortably over the hand. Add approximately 2cm (3/4") ease to the measurement to allow for this.

An open cuff with a fastening can be made to fit more tightly. The cuff length should be a looser measurement taken around the wrist or arm where the cuff is required to fit. Draw a rectangle for this length plus 3cm (11/8") for the fastening wrap by the width of the cuff. Shape the cuff end as required.

When the cuff is wider than 3cm (11/8"), the sleeve is shortened to allow for a set amount of 'blousing' over the cuff.
The amount to be cut from the sleeve length is calculated from the finished width of the cuff minus 2cm (3/4"). That is, if the width of the cuff is 6cm (23/8"), then only 4cm (11/2") is cut off the sleeve length. The more fullness required to blouse over the cuff the less is cut off the sleeve.

Mark the sleeve opening position at Q on line C-E on the back sleeve wristline. Mark up 6cm (23/8") for the opening which can be finished with a narrow hem or else a placket pattern can be made.

Interfacing must be put into the cuff to give it firmness and to reinforce the buttonholes and buttons.

Shirt sleeve

1. Mark the sleeve opening position at Q on line C-E on the back sleeve wristline. Mark up 6cm (21/2") for the opening.

2. The cuff pattern is made by drawing a rectangle the wrist measurement plus 3cm (11/8") fastening wrap by the width of the cuff.

The cuff can be cut in one piece with a fold or in two pieces. Make a pattern for the interfacing.
Add seam allowance and make corresponding balance marks.
Mark the grain line on all pattern pieces.

 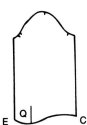 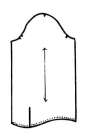

2. TWO PIECE CUFF — Wrist + Wrap / Cut 4 Fabric / Cut 2 Interfacing

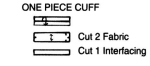

ONE PIECE CUFF — Cut 2 Fabric / Cut 1 Interfacing

Blouse sleeve

1. Mark up from C-E the amount the sleeve seam is to be shortened.
   Make line X-Y parallel to C-E.
   Mark the position of the sleeve opening above Q.

2. Cut through line X-Y.
   Slash from G to H, from Z to B and Z to F.
   Spread line H-Z 1cm (3/8") at Z.
   Raise Z-B and Z-F by 2cm (3/4") for extra height to the sleeve head.

3. Reshape the head of the sleeve to give a more rounded look to the gathers.
   Add seam allowance and make corresponding balance marks.

4. The cuff pattern is made by drawing a rectangle the wrist measurement plus 3cm (11/8") fastening wrap by the width of the cuff.
   The cuff end can be shaped as required.

5. Add seam allowance and make corresponding balance marks.

 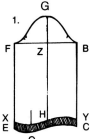 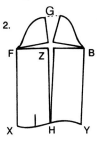 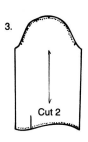 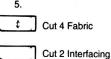

3. Cut 2

5. Cut 4 Fabric / Cut 2 Interfacing

Use the basic sleeve pattern as a foundation for the following.

Full gathered sleeve

This style sleeve is suitable for very fine and sheer fabrics.

1. Mark up from E-C the amount the sleeve seam is to be shortened. Mark line X-Y parallel to the line E-C. Divide the sleeve into 8 equal sections.

2. Cut through line X-Y and then through each section. Spread each section the amount required.

3. Add seam allowance and make corresponding balance marks. Mark the grain line on each pattern piece.

Deep cuff

4. To make the cuff pattern, draw a rectangle the wrist measurement plus 3cm (11/8") fastening wrap by the width of the cuff.
   Divide the cuff into 4 sections.

5. Slash to the wrist and spread to fit the above wrist measurement plus wrap.

6. Add seam allowance and make corresponding balance marks. Mark the grain line on each pattern piece.

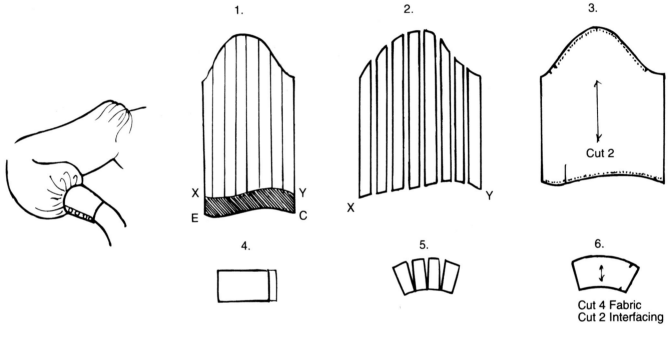

Bell sleeve

1. Divide the sleeve into 8 equal parts.

2. Slash from the wrist to the head of the sleeve and spread evenly. Reshape the end of the sleeve.

3. Add seam allowance and make corresponding balance marks. The sleeve can be finished with a facing. If gathers are required, cut a bias strip for the casing for the elastic. Mark the grain line on each pattern piece.

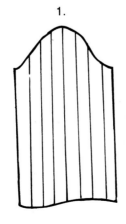
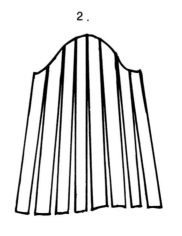
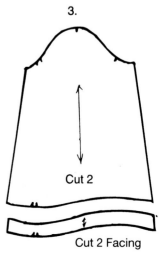

Use the basic sleeve block pattern as a foundation for
the following.

Cape sleeve

1. Mark the length of the sleeve required down from A and B
   to C and D. Cut through line C-D and divide the top part of
   the sleeve into 8 equal sections.

2. Spread line A-B sections by 1.5cm (1/2") and line C-D
   sections by 2cm (3/4").

3. Reshape the head and hem of the sleeve.
   The sleeve can be finished with a narrow rolled hem or a
   separate facing. Gather the head of the sleeve.
   Add seam allowance and make corresponding balance marks.
   Mark the grain line on each pattern piece.

 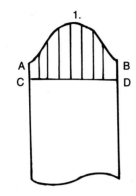  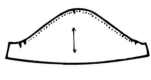

Puff sleeve

This sleeve is drafted as the cape sleeve.

1. Gather the head and the end of the sleeve.

2. Finish the edge with elastic, a bias strip or a fitted band.

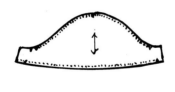 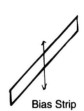 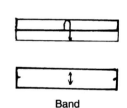

Bias Strip

Band

Bon-bon sleeve

This sleeve is suitable for fine and sheer fabrics.

1. Join C-E with a straight line.
   Divide the sleeve length into 5 equal sections. Mark the
   position for the puff gathers between E-F and C-D.

2. Cut the pattern from head to hem and spread to the required
   fullness.
   Add wrist frill width to the sleeve length.

3. The hem frill can be finished with lace or a rolled hem.
   The sleeve puffs can be gathered up with shirring elastic or
   narrow elastic. Gather the head of the sleeve into the
   armhole.
   Add seam allowance and make corresponding balance marks.
   Mark the grain line on each pattern piece.

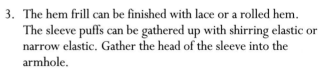

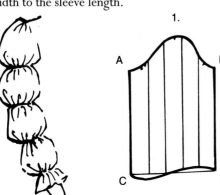 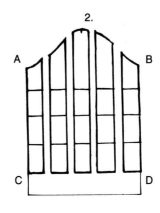 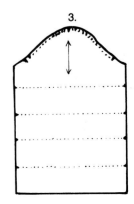

Use the basic block patterns of the sleeve and front and back bodice drafts as a foundation for the following.

Magyar sleeve

1. Place the shoulders of the front and back bodices together at the neck at A and 2cm (3/4") apart at B.

2. Place the centre of the sleeve head 1cm (3/8") above point B.
    Pivot the sleeve at B until D is an equal distance from E on the front and back bodice.
    Mark down 4cm (11/2") from E to F and D to G.
    Join F to G with a good curve for the new underarm seam.

3. This bodice can be cut in one piece as drafted with either the centre front or back bodice placed on the straight grain.

4. Cut through line A-H to separate the front and back bodices and sleeves.

5. Cut through line G for a short sleeve bodice.
    The centre front and back can be placed on the fold or seamed.
    The sleeve can be tapered with the end hemmed, elasticised or gathered into the bias strip or a cuff.
    Add seam allowance and make corresponding balance marks.
    Mark the grain line on each pattern piece.

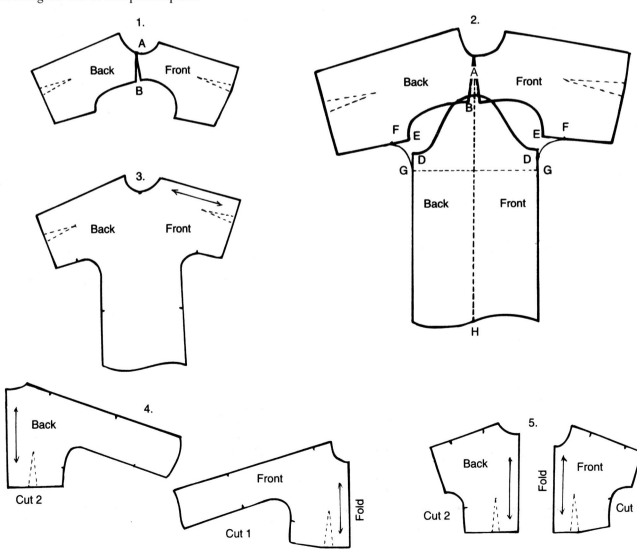

Use the basic block patterns of the sleeve and front and back bodice drafts as a foundation for the following.

Raglan sleeve

The raglan is an easy fitting sleeve which is constructed with the shoulder seam moved towards the front.

1. Place the shoulders of the front and back bodices together at the neck and armhole. Move the shoulder line 1cm (3/8") towards the front to line A-B.

2. Mark down 2cm (3/4") from A to C on the front bodice and A to D on the back bodice.
    Mark up 8cm (31/8") from E to F on the front bodice and G to H on the back bodice. Join C to F and D to H with a curved line.

3. Cut through A to B for the new shoulder line and C to F and D to H to separate the shoulder sections from the bodices.

4. Move the centre of the head of the sleeve 1cm (3/8") towards the front at I. Mark 3cm (11/8") down from I for J.
    Mark 1cm (3/8") each side of I for K on the front and L on the back sleeve. Join K to N and L to M with a curved line.
    Mark down 4cm (11/2") from M to O and N to P.

5. Slash from M to L and N to K and raise N and M 3cm (11/8") to join M to O and N for the new underarm seam.
    Place the shoulder sections in position with front armhole section B-F on line K-F-E and the back B-H on line L-H-G.
    Keep line C-F-E and D-H-G a smooth line. Join A-J-A for the shoulder dart.

6. The sleeve can be cut in one piece with a shoulder dart or cut in two pieces   with a shoulder seam from R to the end of the sleeve which can be short or long.
    Keep a smooth line at R.
    Add hem and seam allowance and make corresponding balance marks. Mark the grain line on each pattern.

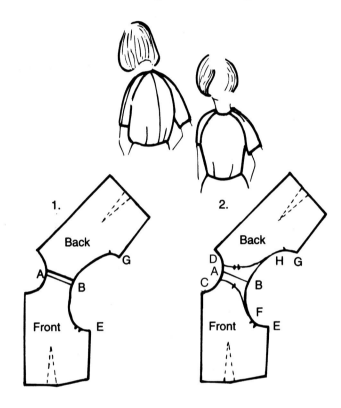

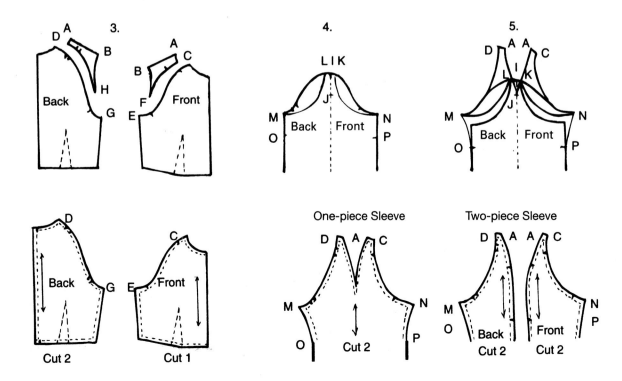

Basic skirt block draft

This basic skirt draft is the block pattern used as a foundation for the skirt pattern designs in this book. The front and back skirt have been drafted together for convenience and can be separated at line G-F.

A straight skirt is rarely worn by children so fullness must be added to the hemline to allow for movement.

Skirts are impractical for small children unless the waist is elasticised or held up with straps or a pinafore top. This is because there is very little difference between the waist and the hip measurement in the smaller sizes to keep the skirt firmly in position.

There are no waist darts in the small (2-4-6) sizes as small children tend to have a large stomach and a thicker waistline. The front skirt is 2cm (3/4") wider than the back skirt to ensure

that the side seam lies in the correct position. This corresponds to the waistline of the front and back bodice block draft.

4cm (11/2") ease has been allowed around the waist in this draft.

6cm (21/2") ease has been allowed around the hips in this draft.

The skirt length taken from the back waist to the knees is a body measurement and not a fashion one. This can be easily adjusted by shortening the skirt to the required length.

Personal measurements can be substituted for those on the chart. For imperial version see p83.

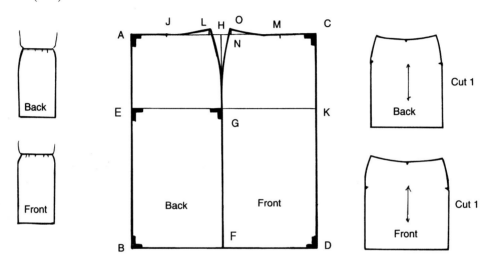

		Children		Girls				Centimetres
Size	2	4	6	8	10	12	14	
A-B	27	32	37	42	47	52	57	Skirt length from back waist. Square out from A to B.
A-C	31	34	36	39	42	45	48	Half hip measurement plus ease. Square down to D.
A-E	10	12	14	15	16	17	18	Down from waist to hipline. Square across to E.
E-G	15	16.25	17.5	19	20.5	22	23.5	Half A-C minus 1cm. Square up to H and down to F.
A-J	6	6.5	7	7.5	8	8.5	9	Equals B-U on back bodice.
J-L	8	8.5	9	10	10.5	11	11.5	Equals U-W on back bodice.
K-L	0.5	0.5	0.5	1	1	1	1	Mark up from K.
A-L								Join back waistline with a curve.
C-M	6	6.5	7	7.5	8	8.5	9	Equals E-V on the front bodice.
M-N	9	9.5	10	11	11.5	12	12.5	Equals V-X on the front bodice.
N-O	0.5	0.5	0.5	1	1	1	1	
C-O								Join with a curve for the front waistline.
L-G								Shape with a curve for the hipline.
O-G								Shape with a curve for the hipline.

This completes the basic front and back draft for sizes 2-4-6.
Separate the front and back skirt through the side seam line G-F.
The centre front and back pattern can be placed on the fold or seamed.
Add seam allowance and make corresponding balance marks.
Mark the grain line on each pattern piece.

Basic skirt block draft with darts

The following waist dart construction gives a more fitted
waistline for sizes 8-10-12-14. For imperial version see p83.

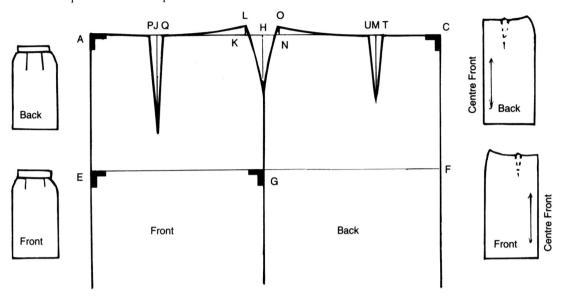

	Children			Girls				Centimetres
Size	2	4	6	8	10	12	14	
J-R				1	12	13	14	Back length dart.
J-P				1	1.25	1.5	1.75	Half back dart width.
J-Q				1	1.25	1.5	1.75	Half back dart width. Join P-R-Q for back dart.
M-S				9	9.5	10	10.5	Front dart length.
M-T				1	1.25	1.5	1.75	Half front dart width.
M-U				1	1.25	1.5	1.75	Half front dart width. Join T-S-U for front dart.

This completes the construction of the basic skirt draft which is
used as a foundation for the other skirt styles.
Separate the front and the back skirt at the side seam line G-I.
The centre front and back can be placed on the fold or seamed.
Add seam allowance and make corresponding balance marks.
Mark the grain line on each pattern piece.

Waistband

To make a waistband pattern, draw a rectangle the width of the
band by the waist measurement plus 4cm (11/2") allowance for
the fastening wrap.
If required, interlining or interfacing can be used to give
firmness to the waistband.

1. The waistband can be cut in one piece with a fold on the top
   edge.

2. The waistband can be cut in two pieces with a seam. This can
   also be used for the interfacing pattern.

3. Add seam allowance and make corresponding balance marks.
   Mark the grain line on each pattern piece.

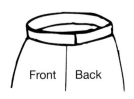

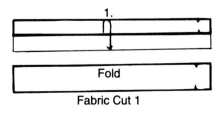

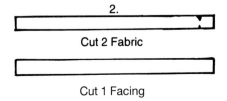

Skirt patterns

The basic skirt block draft is a straight skirt and is rarely worn by children in the draft form. Flare should be added to the hemline to allow for movement.

Use the basic skirt draft as a foundation for the following.

Flared two-piece skirt

1. Mark out from I on the front and back side seam approximately 2.5cm (1") for sizes 2-6 and 4cm (11/2") for sizes 8-10-12-14.
   Join V to G at the hipline.
   Make line G-V at the same length as G-I.
   Join V-I with a slight curve to the hemline.

2. Add seam and hem allowance and make corresponding balance marks.
   Place the centre front and back on the fold.
   Mark the grain line on each pattern piece.

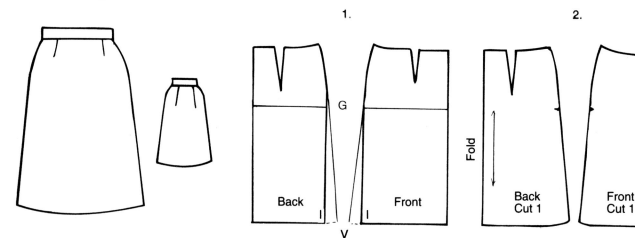

Skirt with an inverted pleat

This is the simplest method of preparing a pattern for pleats in the centre front or back of a skirt.
Use a flared 2-piece or 4-gore skirt pattern as a foundation for the following.

1. Pleat the pattern paper as required. Lay the skirt pattern in position and trace around it.

2. Add seam and hem allowance and make corresponding balance marks.
   Indicate the direction of the pleats.
   Place line C-D on the fold.
   Mark the grain line on each pattern piece.

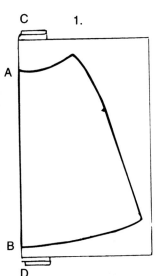

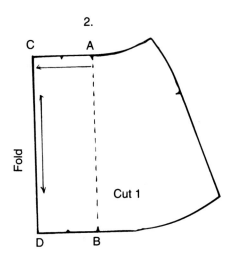

Four-gore skirt

Use the basic front and back skirt block patterns as a foundation for the following.

1. Draw a line parallel to the centre front and back line from the end of the darts at A to B at the hemline.

2. Slash from B to A and spread the hemline the amount required.
   Join B to C with a curve.

3. Add seam and hem allowance and make corresponding balance marks.
   The centre front and back can be placed on the straight or bias grain which spreads the fullness evenly around the body.
   Mark the grain line on each pattern piece.

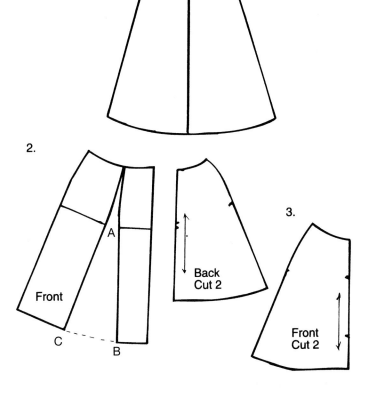

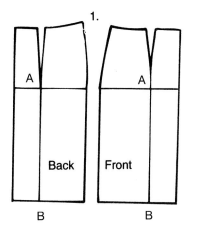

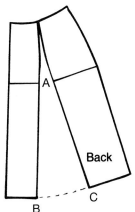

Multi-gore skirt

A multi-gore skirt is the simplest to assemble when each panel is identical.
This style of skirt is more suitable for sizes 8-10-12-14.

1. Add 4cm (11/2") ease to the waist measurement and divide by the number of gores required.
   Draft the pattern by drawing a rectangle using this measurement by the length of the skirt A-E and B-F.
   Measure down approximately 17cm (65/8") from the waistline A-B to the hipline C-D.

2. Slash from hem to waist.
   Add 6cm (23/8") ease to the hip measurement and divide by the number of gores required.
   Spread the hip line C-D to this measurement.
   Join the hemline with a curve.

3. Add seam and hem allowance and make corresponding balance marks.
   Mark the grain line on each pattern piece.

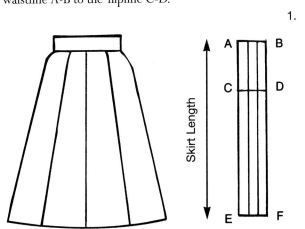

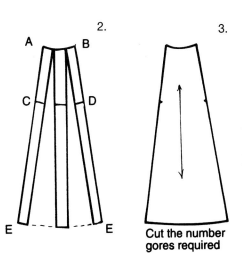

Half-circle skirt

1. Draft the pattern by marking a rectangle half the waist measurement by the skirt length. Divide the pattern into 5 equal sections.

2. Slash from hem to waist and spread each section the same distance working from A in the centre of a straight line. Reshape the hemline.

Place line D-E on the fold. Seam line B-C can be placed on the selvedge.

3. Add seam and hem allowance and make corresponding balance marks. Mark the grain line on each pattern piece.

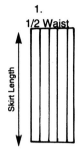
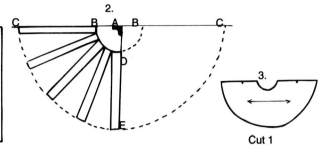

Circle skirt

1. Draft the pattern by marking a rectangle half the waist measurement by the skirt length.
   Divide the pattern into 5 equal sections.

2. Slash from hem to waist and spread each section an even distance from A. Reshape the hemline.
   Seam line B-C can be placed on the selvedge.

3. Add seam and hem allowance and make corresponding balance marks. Mark the grain line on each pattern piece.

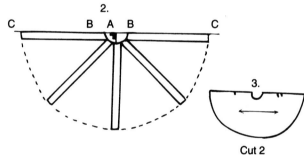

Half-circle skirt with gathers

1. Draft the pattern by marking a rectangle half the waist measurement by the skirt length.
   Divide the pattern into 5 equal sections.

2. Draw a straight line and make a right angle down from A. Mark a quarter circle approximately 20cm (8") down from A to B.

3. Cut through each section of the skirt and spread evenly as shown.
   Reshape the hemline.

Line D-E is placed on the fold.
Seam line B-C can be placed on the selvedge.
Add seam and hem allowance and make corresponding balance marks. Mark the grain line on each pattern piece.

Note
This skirt can be marked directly on to the fabric and cut out by pivoting down 20cm (8") from A to B. Mark the skirt length from B to C.

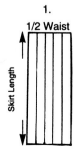
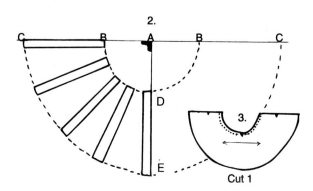

Gathered skirt

A simple gathered skirt is suitable for children who need a little shaping in their clothes. The amount of fullness required is governed by the type of fabric chosen. Allow approximately 3 times the waist measurement for fine fabrics and twice the waist measurement for thicker fabrics. An easy way to check how much you need is to run two rows of gathering threads from selvedge to selvedge. Draw the threads to the desired amount, hold against the figure and adjust if necessary.
If gathers are not suitable for the fabric, then consider unpressed pleats which will be less bulky.
Except for commercial use, a pattern is not necessary for a simple gathered, tiered or pleated skirt. The measurement can be made directly onto fabric and cut out. A strip of paper approximately 10cm (4 1/4") wide on which pleating fold notches can be marked is a useful guide.

Whichever method is used, remember to add seam and hem allowances and to make corresponding balance marks.
Mark the grain line on each pattern piece.

Draft the skirt pattern by making a rectangle approximately 3 times the waist measurement by the skirt length.
Add seam and hem allowance and make corresponding balance marks. Mark the grain line on each pattern piece.
Sew in two rows of gathering at the waistline and draw into the waist measurement.

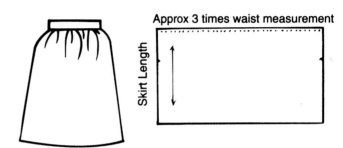

Approx 3 times waist measurement

Skirt Length

Gathered tiered skirt

The amount of fullness and the number of tiers varies depending on the design of the skirt.
Divide the skirt length into the number of tiers required.
This will establish the width of each tier.
The length of the waist tier is approximately 1.5 times the waist measurement.
The length of the centre tier is approximately 3 times the waist measurement.

The length of the hem tier is approximately 6 times the waist measurement.
Add seam allowance and hem allowance and make corresponding balance marks.
Mark the grain line on each pattern piece.

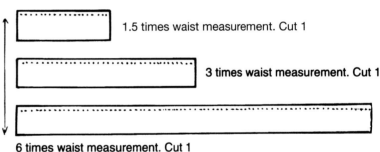

1.5 times waist measurement. Cut 1

3 times waist measurement. Cut 1

6 times waist measurement. Cut 1

Skirt with hem frill or flounce

This skirt has a wide frill or flounce at the hemline.

Use a flared or 4-gore skirt as a foundation for this skirt.

1. Mark down from the waistline the length of the skirt required. Draw a line parallel to the hemline.
   Cut through this line and discard the hem section.

2. Measure around the new hemline and multiply by three for the length of the frilling required by the width of the flounce.

   Add seam allowance and make corresponding balance marks. Mark the grain line on each pattern piece.

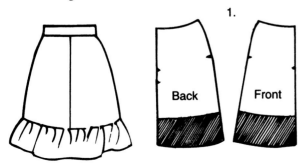

1.

Back   Front

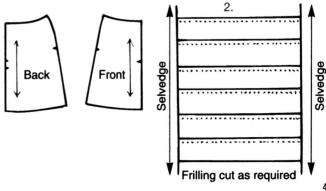

Back   Front

2.

Selvedge   Selvedge

Frilling cut as required

Skirt with hip yoke and gathers

Use the basic front and back skirt block patterns as a foundation for the following.

1. Mark down from the waistline the depth of the yoke required on the front and back skirt patterns.

2. Cut through the yoke line and close the waist darts.

3. Measure around the hip line of the yoke and draw the skirt pattern approximately 3 times this measurement by the length of the skirt required.

4. Add seam and hem allowance and make corresponding balance marks.
   Mark the grain line on each pattern piece.

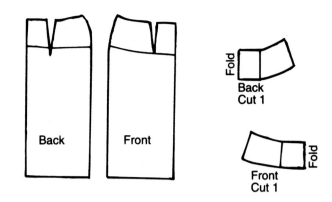

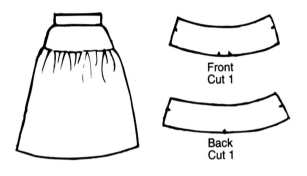

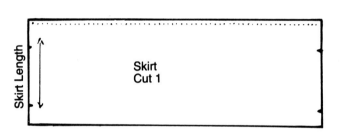

Skirt with hip yoke and pleats
Refer to page 9 for information on pleating.

Knife pleats

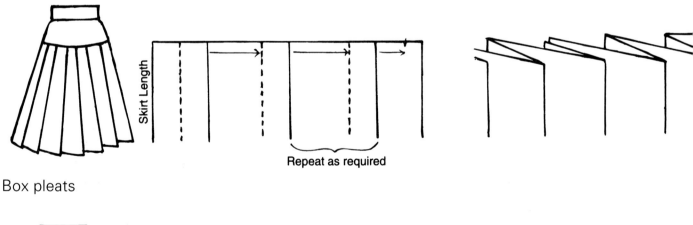

Box pleats

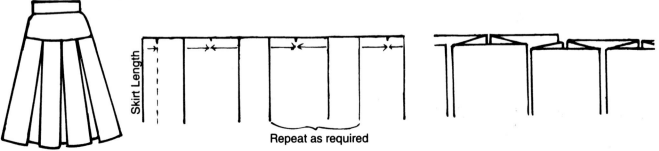

Fitted knife-pleated skirt

These tapered pleats are more suitable for larger sizes where there is a greater difference between the waist and hip measurements.

Calculate the difference between the waist and hip measurements and divide this amount by the number of pleats. This will give the amount each pleat must be tapered or overlapped. Tack the pleats from the hem to the hipline before adjusting the waist pleats.

Stitch each pleat from the waist to the hipline to hold it in place.

Add seam and hem allowance and indicate the direction the pleats face.

Mark the grain line on each pattern piece.

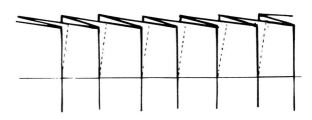

Kilt

A kilt is a wrap skirt with an adjustable waistline.

Its construction is similar to the fitted knife-pleated skirt with an unpleated upper and under wrap.

The fabric required is calculated by the number and width of the pleats required plus the width of the two wraps by the length of the skirt.

The pleats are tapered from the hipline to the waist. Each pleat can be stitched down from the waist to the hipline.

Add seam and hem allowance and indicate the direction the pleats face.

Mark the grain line on each pattern piece.

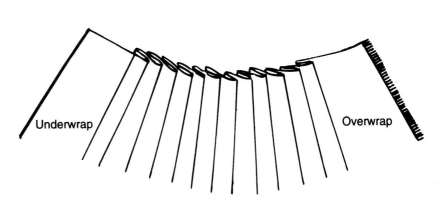

Underwrap

Overwrap

Culottes or divided skirt

Use the basic four-gore skirt pattern as a foundation for the following.

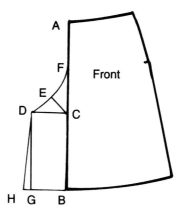

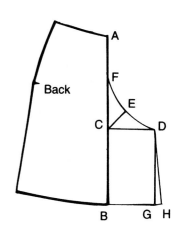

1.

Size	8	10	12	14	Centimetres
Front					
A-B	42	47	52	57	Required skirt length.
A-C	26	27	28	29	Body rise or crotch depth. Square across from C.
C-D	9	9.75	10.5	11.25	1/8 hip measurement. Bisect angle A-C-D.
C-E	5	5.25	5.5	5.75	Half C-D plus 0.5cm.
C-F	18	18	18	18	On line A-B.
D-F					Join D-E-F with a curve for the fork section.
G-H	2	2	2	2	Pivot out 2cm from G to H. Join H to D. D-H equals B-C.
Back					
A-B	42	47	52	57	Required skirt length.
A-C	26	27	28	29	Body rise or crotch depth. Square across from C.
C-D	13	13.75	14.5	15.25	1/8 hip measurement plus 4cm.
C-E	6.5	6.75	7	7.25	Half C-D.
C-F	18	18	18	18	On line A-B.
D-F					Join D-E-F with a curve for the fork section. Square down from D to G.
G-H	2	2	2	2	Pivot out 2cm from G-H. Join H to D. D-H equals B-C.

2.

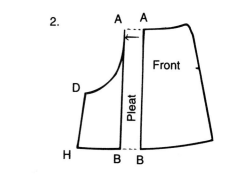

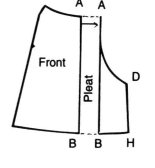

3.

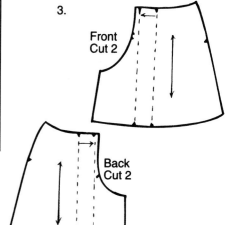

2. To draft the inverted pleat, separate the crotch section on the front and back skirt patterns at A-B. Move this section out the width of the pleat by 8cm (3 1/8") for sizes 8-10 and 10cm (4") for sizes 12-14.

3. Add seam and hem allowance and make corresponding balance marks. Mark the grain line on each pattern piece. Mark the direction of the pleats.

Basic dress block draft

This simple A-line dress block can be adapted for many styles.
It is designed as a flattering and comfortable style for an active girl and disguises the thick waistline of a small child.
It has a raised waistline approximately midway between the waist and the armhole and a gentle flare to the hemline.
The amount of flare at the hemline will vary according to fashion and preference. It is recommended that 6cm (2 3/8") should be allowed for sizes 2-4-6, 8cm (3 1/8") for sizes 8-10 and 10cm (4") for 12-14.
This dress can be any length.
Use the basic front and back bodice drafts as a foundation for the following.

1. Place the centre front and back bodices 2cm (3/4") apart with the chest A-B in line.
   Trace around these block patterns.
   Mark the centre back dress length from C to D and square across.
   Mark the centre front dress length from E to F and square across.
   The construction of the front and back dress block draft is identical from this point on.
   Square down from G on line A-B through the centre of the dart to H on the hemline.
   K is half the side seam length B-J.
   Square down from K to L.
   Make line K-L on the front pattern the same length as on the back pattern to equalize the side seam length.
   Pivot line K-L out the same amount of flare required to M.
   Join M to L.

Curve the side seam at K for a smoother line.
Join H to M to complete the hemline.

2. Add seam and hem allowance and make corresponding balance marks.
   Mark the grain lines on each pattern piece.
   Centre front and back can be placed on the fold or seamed.

1.

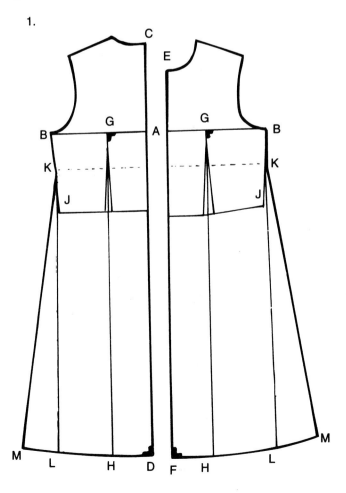

2.

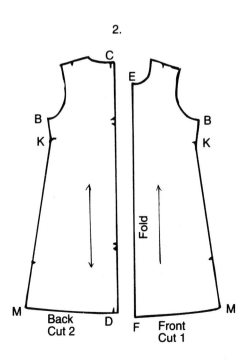

Dress patterns

Use the basic dress block patterns as a foundation for
the following.

Panel dress

1. Halve the shoulder line at R and join to S at the top of the
   dart with a slight curve.
   Draw a line S-H parallel to the centre back line C-D and
   centre front line E-F.
   Mark T and V 1cm (3/8") each side of H for sizes 2-4-6 and
   2cm (3/4") for sizes 8-10-12-14. Join T and V to S for the
   new seam lines.

2. It is necessary to separate each pattern piece as the ends of
   the skirt panels overlap at the hemline.

Separate the panel by tracing around the patterns.
Centre back panel is C-D-V-S-R-C.
Back side panel is R-S-T-M-K-B-R.
Centre front panel is E-F-V-S-R-E.
Front side panel is R-S-T-M-K-B-R.
Add seam and hem allowance and make corresponding
balance marks.
Mark the grain lines on each pattern piece.
Centre front and back can be placed on the fold or seamed.

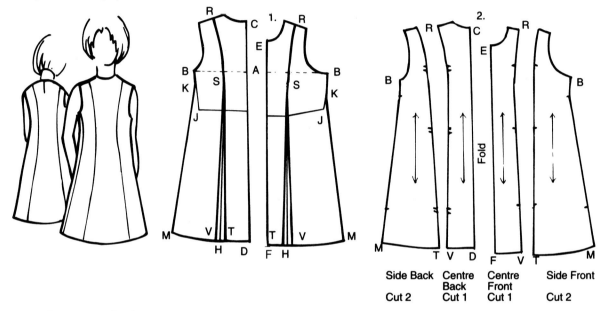

Side Back — Cut 2 · Centre Back — Cut 1 · Centre Front — Cut 1 · Side Front — Cut 2

Shaped panel dress

1. P is half the armhole depth B-N.
   Join P to S at the top of the dart with a curve.

2. Separate the panel by tracing off the pattern as below.
   Centre back panel is C-D-V-S-P-N-C.
   Back side panel is P-S-T-M-K-B-P.
   Centre front panel is E-F-V-S-P-N-E.

Front side panel is P-S-T-M-K-B-P.
Add seam and hem allowance and make corresponding
balance marks. Mark the grain lines on each pattern piece.
Centre front and back can be placed on the fold or seamed.

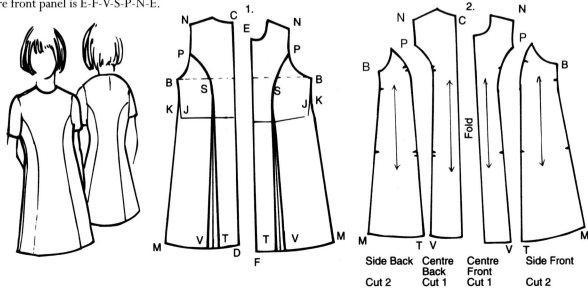

Side Back — Cut 2 · Centre Back — Cut 1 · Centre Front — Cut 1 · Side Front — Cut 2

Use the basic dress block patterns as a foundation for the following.

Princess line dress

This fitted style is more suitable for an older girl in the larger sizes 8-10-12-14.

1. Halve the shoulder line at R and join to G at the top of the dart with a slight curve.
   Mark the amount of the flare required each side of H at X and Y.
   Make lines V-Y and W-X equal to the measurement from H to the waistline.
   Join B to J and curve to M for a more fitted waistline.

2. Each pattern piece has to be separated as the ends of the skirt panels overlap at the hemline.
   Separate each panel by tracing around the patterns as below.
   Centre back panel is C-D-Y-V-G-R-C.
   Back side panel is R-G-W-X-M-B-R.
   Centre front panel is E-F-Y-V-G-R-E.
   Front side panel is R-G-W-X-M-B-R.

Add seam and hem allowance and make corresponding balance marks.
Mark the grain lines on each pattern piece.
Centre front and back can be cut on the fold or seamed.

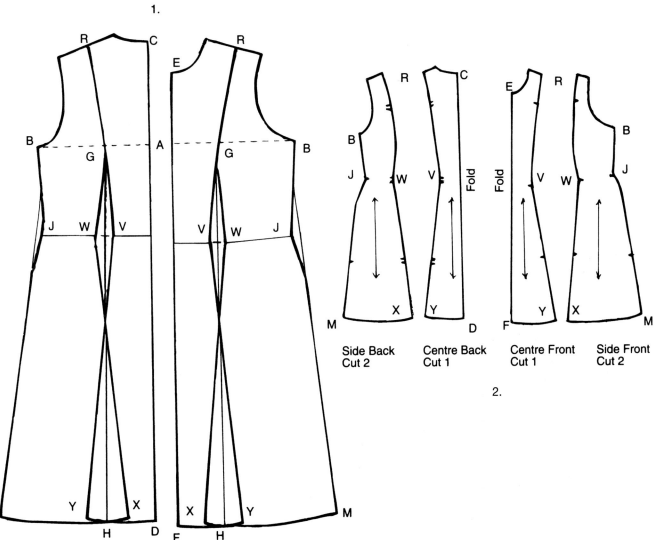

Side Back
Cut 2

Centre Back
Cut 1

Centre Front
Cut 1

Side Front
Cut 2

1.

2.

Basic trouser block draft

This basic trouser block draft can be used for all children as girls and boys have the same measurements at sizes 2-4-6.
Separate blocks may be necessary for sizes 8-10-12-14 due to their different shape. Boys have a flatter stomach and do not need tucks or darting at the front. Older boys have a slightly larger waist and narrower hips than girls. Therefore the back dart can be shorter in the boys draft to account for higher buttocks. The draft for sizes 8-10-12-14 can be used for boys with these simple adjustments:
4cm (1 1/2") ease allowed around the waist.
6cm (2 3/8") ease allowed around the hips.
Personal measurements can be substituted for those on the chart. The leg length and measurements given for the knee and hem widths canvary to suit individual requirements. For imperial version see p88.

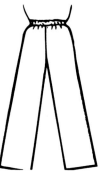

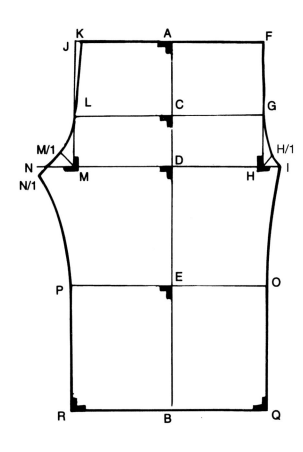

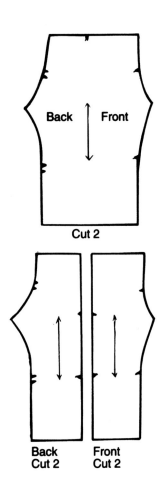

Back — Front
Cut 2

Back
Cut 2

Front
Cut 2

	Children			Girls & Boys				Centimetres
Size	2	4	6	8	10	12	14	
A-B	46	54	62	70	78	86	94	Side seam length from back waist to ankle. Square out each side of A and B.
A-C	10	12	14	15	16	17	18	Waist to hip. Square out each side of C.
A-D	19	21	23	25	27	29	31	Body rise plus ease. Square out each side of D.
D-E	13	16	19	20	22	28	31	Knee line half D-B. Square out.
A-F	15.5	16.75	18	19.5	21	22.5	24	1/4 hip measurement plus ease. Square down to G and H.
H-I	3	3.75	4	4.5	5	5.5	6	
H-H/1	2.25	2.5	2.75	3	3.25	3.5	3.75	Bisect angle G-H-I.
F-I								Join F-G-H/1-I for centre front seam.
A-J	15.5	16.75	18	19.5	21	22.5	24	1/4 hip measurement plus ease. Square down L and M.
J-K	0.5	0.75	1	1.5	1.75	2	2.25	Back seam suppression. Join to L.
M-N	7	7.5	8	8.5	9	9.5	10	
M-M/1	3	3.5	4	4.5	4.75	5	5.25	Bisect angle L-M-N.
N-N/1	0.5	0.5	0.5	1	1	1	1	Mark down from N.
K-N/1								Join K-L-M/1-N/1 for centre back seam.
E-O	16	17	18	20	22	24	26	1/2 knee measurement plus ease. Square down to Q.
E-P	16	17	18	20	22	24	26	1/2 knee measurement plus ease. Square down to R.

The above draft is ideal for the smallest sizes (2-4-6) as it is not necessary to have either side seams or waist darts due to the slightness of the variation between the waist and hip measurements.
The trousers can be cut in two pieces or, if a side seam is required, cut through line A-B.
This draft can be used for all sizes where elasticised waistline is required for comfort such as in track suit pants and pyjamas.
Add seam allowance and make corresponding balance marks.
Mark the grain line on each pattern piece.

The following draft gives a fitted waistline for the larger sizes 8-10-12-14. This will construct the front and back darts.
If preferred, a front tuck W-X can replace the dart.
Face the tuck towards the side seam.
For imperial version see p89.

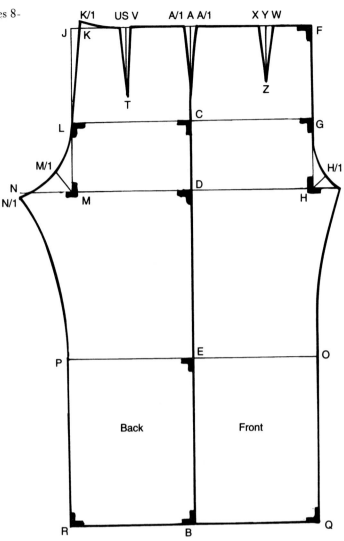

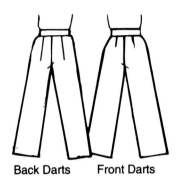

Back Darts   Front Darts

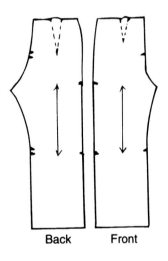

Back   Front

	Children			**Girls & Boys**				Centimetres
Size	2	4	6	8	10	12	14	
K-K/1				1	1.25	1.5	1.75	Extend line L-K above line J-F. Join K to a with a curve.
A-A/1				0.5	1	1.5	2	Mark each side of A. Join to C with a curve.
K/1-S				7.5	8	8.5	9	Join with a curve.
S-U				0.75	1	1.25	1.5	Half back dart width.
S-V				0.75	1	1.25	1.5	Half back dart width.
S-T			Girls	11	12	13	14	Back dart length. Join U-T-V for back dart.
			Boys	9.5	10.5	11.5	12.5	Back dart length. Join U-T-V for back dart.
F-W				6.5	7	7.5	8	
W-X				3	3.5	4	4.5	Front tuck width.
	for front darts only			**Girls**				
W-Y				1.5	1.75	2	2.25	Half front dart width.
Y-X				1.5	1.75	2	2.25	Half front dart width.
Y-Z				9	9.5	10	10.5	Front dart length. Join W-Z-X for front dart.

Front Tucks

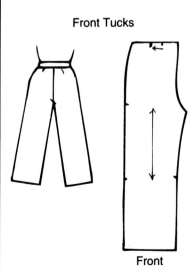

Front

Separate the draft at line A-B for the side seam.
Add seam allowance and make corresponding balance marks. Mark grain lines.

Trouser patterns

Use the basic front and back block patterns without the darts as a foundation for the following.
The pattern can be cut in one piece without a side seam if required.

Boxer style pants and shorts

1. On both front and back patterns mark down from A at the waistline the length of the side seam required for either shorts or pants.
   Add seam and hem allowance and make corresponding balance marks.
   Mark the grain line on each pattern piece.
   The waistline is elasticised for comfort.

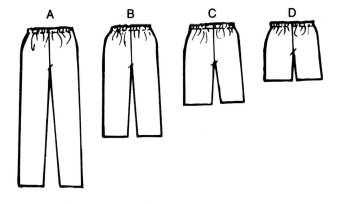

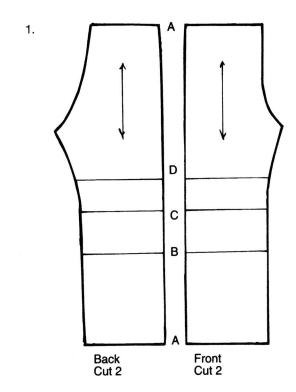

Trousers with turn-ups

1. Mark down from B-C twice the turn-up width.

2. Add seam and hem allowance and make corresponding balance marks. Mark the grain line on each pattern piece.

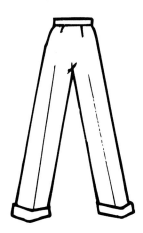

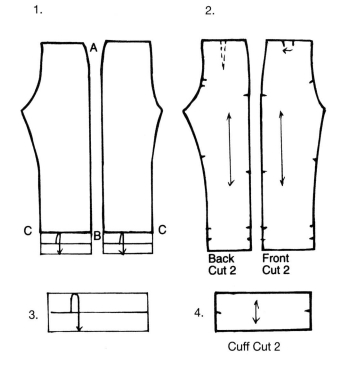

Trousers with separate cuffs

3. Measure the end of the front and back pant leg and draw a rectangle of this measurement by the width of the cuff required.

4. Add seam allowance and make corresponding balance marks. Mark the grain line on each pattern piece.

Use the basic trouser block patterns as a foundation
for the following.

Tapered trousers

The amount to be tapered is an approximate measurement, but
2cm (3/4") from each seam for sizes 8 and 10 and 3cm (11/8")
for sizes 12 and 14 is recommended so that the foot can be easily
pulled through the hem of the trousers.

1. Taper the inside leg and side seam evenly at the hemline at A
   and B.
   Join A to C at the kneeline and B to D at the hipline.

2. Add seam and hem allowance and make corresponding
   balance marks. Mark the grain line on each pattern piece.

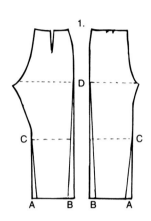
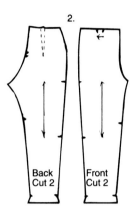

Bermuda-length shorts

These shorts taper to the leg above the knee.

1. Mark the length of the shorts approximately 8cm (31/8")
   above the knee for A and B.
   Measure the leg circumference and add 5cm (2") ease for
   movement.

Taper the inside leg and side seam evenly at A and B.
Join A to C and B to D at the hipline.

2. Add seam and hem allowance and make corresponding
   balance marks. Mark the grain line on each pattern piece.

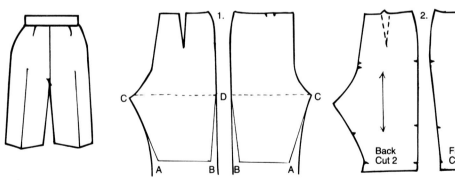

Basic shorts

1. Mark down approximately 7cm (23/4") from A to B and 4cm
   (11/2") from C to D. Join B to D with a slight curve.

2. Add seam and hem allowance and make corresponding
   balance marks. Mark the grain on each pattern piece.

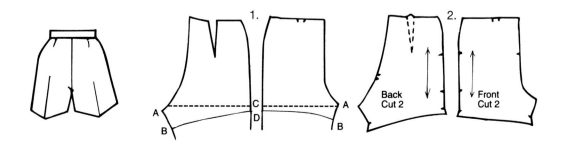

Use the basic trouser block as a foundation for the following.

Flared trousers

1. Straighten the inside leg of the front and back pattern from A to B.
   Add half the remainder of the required flare to the front and back hemline at C on the side seam.
   Join C to D at the hipline with a smooth line.

2. Add seam and hem allowances and make corresponding balance marks.
   Mark the grain line on each pattern piece.

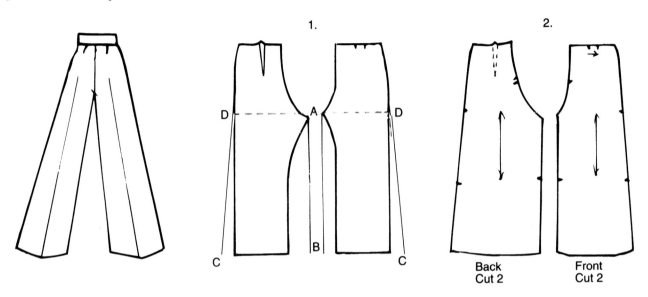

Gaucho pants

1. Mark the length required down from the waist at the side seam.
   Straighten the inside leg of the front and back patterns from A to B.
   Add half the remainder of the required flare to the front and back hemline at C on the side seam.
   Join C to D at the hipline with a smooth line.

2. Add seam and hem allowance and make corresponding balance marks.
   Mark the grain line on each pattern piece.

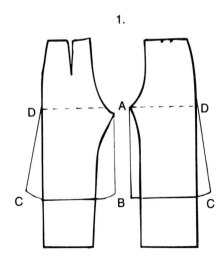
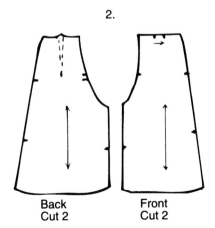

Jean-style trousers

Front

1. Mark the position of the pocket from A on the waistline to B at the side seam. Join A to B with a curve.
   Mark around the hand from C to D for a comfortable pocket shape.
   Mark from F at the centre front waistline approximately 4cm (11/2") to G for the fly fastening facing width. F-H is the fly depth.

2. Trace around C-E-D-C for the pocket.
   Trace around A-B-D-C for the pocket lining.

Trace around F-G-H for the fly facing.
Place F-H on the fold for the front fly placket.
Cut through line A-B for the front pocket edge.

Back

3. Mark the position of the back yoke on the pattern.

4. Cut through this yoke line and close the back dart.

5. Add seam allowance and hem allowance and make corresponding balance marks. Mark the grain line on each pattern piece.

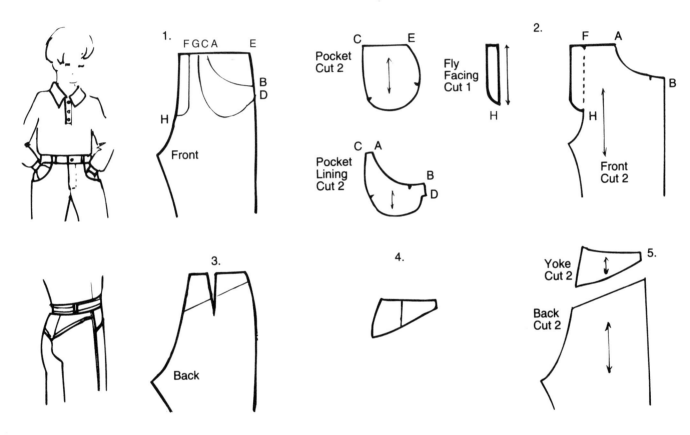

Fly-opening trousers

1. Girls' front fly opening faces towards the left, similar to front bodice openings.

2. Boys' front fly opening faces towards the right, similar to the front shirt openings.

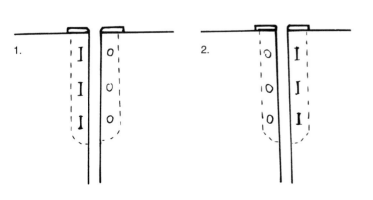

Use the basic front and back trouser and bodice block patterns as a foundation for the following.

A neck opening such as a zipper, front buttoning or a shoulder opening is necessary unless the neckline is large enough to allow the child to step comfortably into the garment.

The full-length garment can be cut in a stretch fabric such as a knitted jersey while woven cotton is suitable for the playsuit.

One-piece suit

1. Extend the centre front and back lines of the trouser pattern. Place the front and back bodices on this line at the waistline. Adjust the side seam if necessary.
   Shape the neck and armholes as required.
   Mark the neck and armhole facing approximately 5cm (2") wide.

2. Add seam and hem allowance and make corresponding balance marks. Mark the grain line on each pattern piece. The centre front and back facing can be placed on the fold to avoid seam bulk at the neckline.

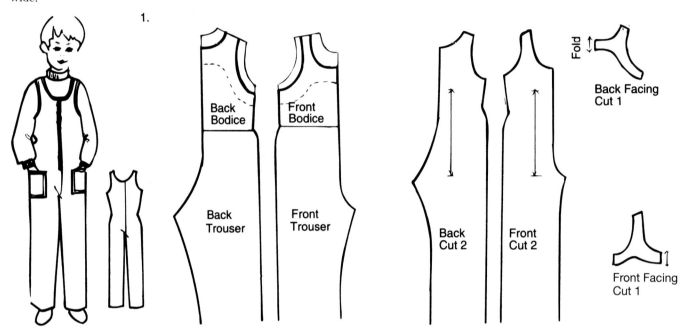

Play suit

1. Extend the centre front and back lines of the trouser pattern. Place the front and back bodices on this line at the waistline. Adjust the side seam if necessary.
   Mark the length of the shorts.
   Shape the neck and armholes as required.
   Add shoulder opening extensions to the front and back bodices.

Mark the neck and armhole facings approximately 5cm (2") wide.

2. Add seam and hem allowance and make corresponding balance marks. Mark the grain line on each pattern piece. Place the centre front and back facing on the fold.

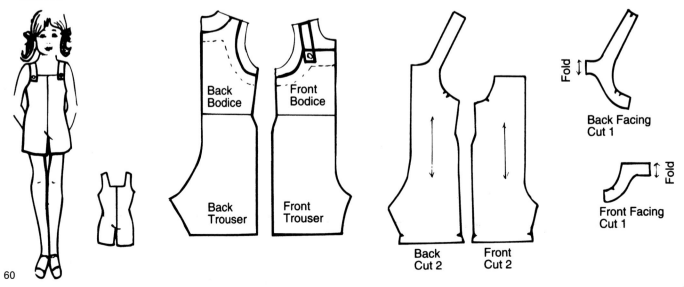

Straps and bib tops

Suspender straps and pinafore and bib tops are ideal to attach to children's trousers, shorts and skirts to hold a shirt or top in place.

The straps can be detachable or attached to the front of the garment. Cross the straps to prevent them from slipping off the shoulders.

Straps must be cut on the straight grain to prevent stretching. Use the basic front and back bodice block as a foundation for the following.

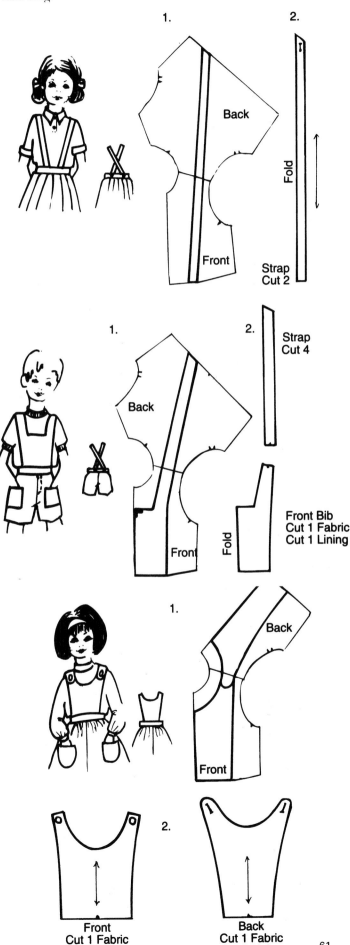

Suspender straps

1. Place the front and full back bodices together at the shoulder. Mark the strap position from the front dart position over the shoulder to the back dart.

   Straps can be made any width but 4cm (1 1/2") is a recommended finished width.

   An alternative method is to measure the child and make the straps longer than required. Adjust the strap length on the figure during a fitting when making the garment.

   An easier method is to use a tape measure over the child from front to back waistline and cut the strap length accordingly.

2. Add seam and fastening allowance to the pattern. Mark the grain line on each pattern piece.

Bib top

1. Place the front and full back bodices together at the shoulder. Mark the position of the bib and straps.

2. Add seam and fastening allowance and make corresponding balance marks. Mark the grain line on each pattern piece. The bib can be cut double or lined.

Pinafore top

1. Place the front and back bodices together at the shoulder. Mark the shape of the top, making the neckline sufficiently large to pull comfortably over the head.

   If the pinafore top is to be attached to trousers or shorts, then a shoulder or centre opening must be allowed to enable the child to step into the garment.

2. Add seam allowance and make corresponding balance marks. The pinafore top can be cut double or lined. Mark the grain line on each pattern piece.

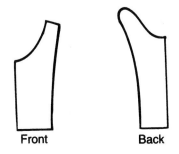

61

Pockets

Pockets add interest to a design and can be made any shape or size. They can be functional, decorative, plain or pleated and finished with top stitching, piping, flaps or a zipper. They may be stitched directly on to the garment or concealed in a seam or panel.

Care must be taken to place functional pockets at a practical angle for easy access.

The position of any pocket must be marked on the garment pattern.

Interfacing can be placed on the pocket edge and into flaps to prevent stretching through constant use.

Pockets are lined in tailored garments.

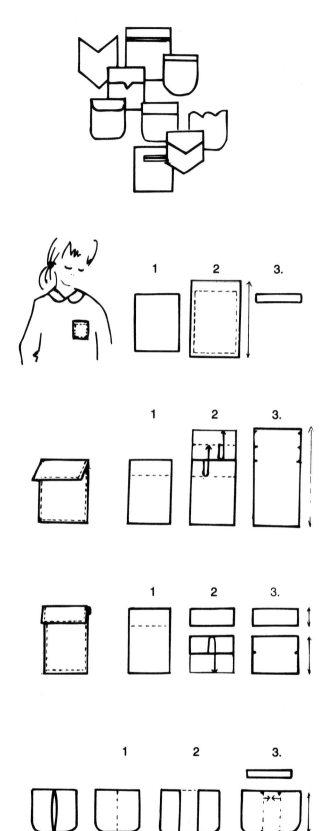

Basic patch pocket

1. Draw a rectangle the size of the pocket required.
2. Add hem and seam allowance and make corresponding balance marks.
3. A strip of interfacing approximately 3cm (11/8") wide can be placed across the top of the pocket in the hem to prevent stretching.
   Mark the grain line on each pattern piece.

Pocket with flap

This pocket has the flap cut in one with the pocket pattern.

1. Draw a rectangle the size of the pocket required.
2. Mark up twice the width of the flap.
3. Add hem and seam allowance and make corresponding balance marks.
   The flap can be interfaced.
   Mark the grain line on each pattern piece.

Pocket with separate flap

1. Draw a rectangle the size of the pocket required.
2. To make the flap pattern, draw a rectangle the width of the pocket by the depth of the flap.
   The flap can be cut in two pieces or placed on the fold and cut in one piece.
3. Add seam allowance and make corresponding balance marks.
   Mark the grain line on each pattern piece.
   The flap can be interfaced.

Pocket with a pleat

1. Draw the pocket the shape and size required.
   Mark the centre of the pocket.
2. Cut and spread the depth of the pleat required.
3. Face the top of the pocket to avoid bulk.
   Add seam allowance and make corresponding balance marks.
   Mark the grain line on each pattern piece.

Inserted pocket

This pocket can be inserted into a seam or a split. It can be concealed or featured with contrast top stitching.

1. Mark around the hand for a comfortable shape.

2. For a concealed pocket, cut 2 paired fabric pieces to allow the pocket to hang loosely inside the garment.

3. To feature the pocket with outside stitching, cut 1 piece of fabric which is stitched directly on to the garment.
   Add seam allowance and make corresponding balance marks.
   Mark the garment pattern for the pocket position.
   Mark the grain line on each pattern piece.

1.

2.

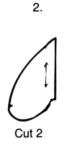

Cut 2

3.

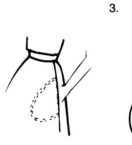

Cut 1

Jeans pocket

1. Mark the position of the pocket from A on the waistline to B at the side seam on the front of the garment.
   Join A-B with a straight or curved line.
   Mark around the hand from C to D for a comfortable shape.

2. Separate the garment at line A-B.

3. Trace around C-E-D-C for the pocket.

4. Trace around A-B-D-C for the pocket lining.
   Add seam allowance and make corresponding balance marks on the garment and pocket.
   Mark the grain line on each pattern piece.

1.   **2.**

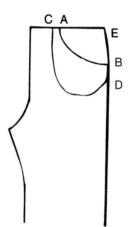

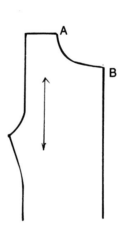

3.

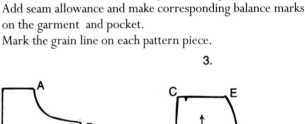

Pocket
Cut 2

4.

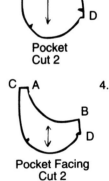

Pocket Facing
Cut 2

1.   **2.**

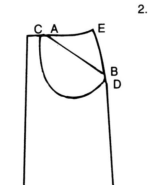

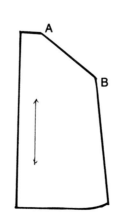

3.

Pocket
Cut 2

4.

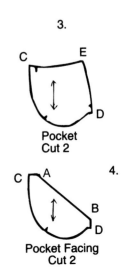

Pocket Facing
Cut 2

Tailored patterns

Use the basic front and back bodices and sleeve block draft patterns as a foundation for the following.
These basic block patterns have to be enlarged so that the jacket can be worn over other garments and be fully lined if required. The following are suggested widths for the fastening wrap to be added to the centre front line:
3cm (11/8") to 4cm (11/2") for a single wrap for all sizes.

8cm (31/8") for a double breasted wrap for sizes 2-4-6.
10cm (4") for a double breasted wrap for sizes 8-10.
12cm (43/4") for a double breasted wrap for sizes 12-14.
The sleeve pattern must be adjusted to fit easily into the enlarged jacket armhole. It must have the extra width throughout its length and the wrist must be kept loose to enable it to be worn comfortably over other sleeves.

Basic jacket block draft

1. Place the centre front and back bodices approximately 8cm (31/8") apart with the chest A-B in line. Trace around the patterns.

Back
C-D Lower the centre back neck 0.5cm (1/4") and draw a line parallel to the neck edge to D on the shoulder line.
D-E Mark out 0.5cm (1/4") from the shoulder point to E and join to D for the new shoulder line.
B-G Lower the armhole 0.5cm (1/4") and move out 1.5cm (1/2") to G.
E-G Reshape the armhole from E to C, utilizing the armhole shape of the block patterns.
C-F Mark the centre back jacket length. Square out from F.
G-H Square down from G to H on the hemline.
F-H Join.

Front
C-D Lower the centre front neck 0.5cm (1/4") and draw a line parallel to the neck edge to D on the shoulder line.
D-E Mark out 0.5cm (1/4") from the shoulder point to E and join to D for new shoulder line.
B-G Lower the armhole 0.5cm (1/4") and out 1.5cm (1/2") to G.
E-G Reshape the armhole from E to G utilizing the armhole shape of the block patterns.
C-F Mark the centre front jacket length. Square out from F.
G-H Square down from G. Make line G-H the same length as line G-H on the back jacket draft to equalize the side seam length.
J-K Square down from line A-B through the centre of the dart to K at the hemline.
F-H Join F-K-H for the front hemline.
L-M Mark the width of the fastening wrap required out from the centre front line C-F to L and M. Join.

Sleeve
2. Trace around the basic sleeve block or the tapered pattern and place on adjacent lines A and B.
   Lower the armhole 0.5cm (1/4") at B and move out 1.5cm (1/2") to D.
   Reshape the head of the sleeve from D to A on the front and back sleeve, utilizing the sleeve block armhole shape.
   Mark the new sleeve seam from D to E parallel to B-C.
   Adjust the length of the sleeve if required.
   Reshape the wristline if necessary on line E-E.

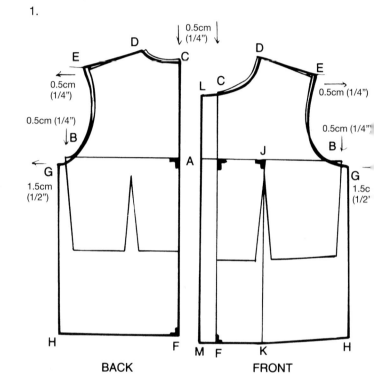

BACK   FRONT

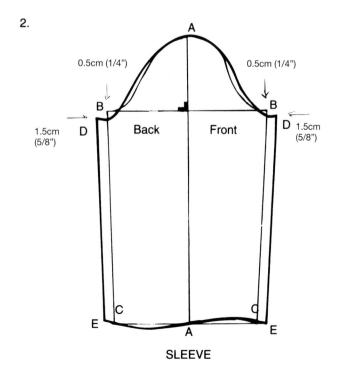

SLEEVE

3. Mark the position of the front and back neck facings.

4. If a lining is required, then cut a pattern to the jacket body and sleeve patterns minus the front and back neck facings. The lining patterns are cut to the finished length of the jacket body and sleeve hems. When hemmed, the lining will be shorter than the jacket.

5. Trace off the facing and interfacing patterns.
   Add seam and hem allowance and make corresponding balance marks.
   Mark the grain line on each pattern piece.
   Any collar and lapel shape can be adapted for the basic jacket block.
   The basic tailored collar pattern can be drafted onto this jacket pattern.

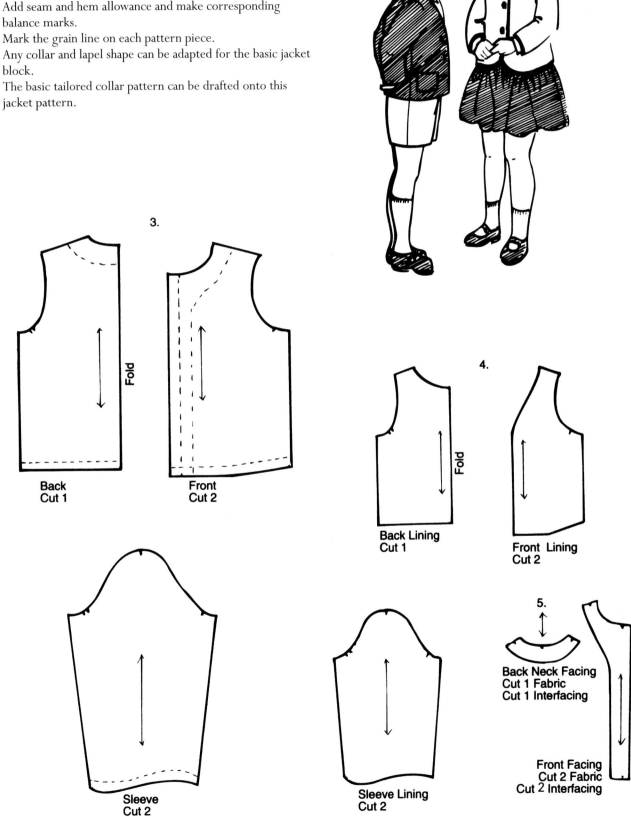

3.

Back
Cut 1

Front
Cut 2

Fold

4.

Back Lining
Cut 1

Front Lining
Cut 2

Fold

Sleeve
Cut 2

Sleeve Lining
Cut 2

5.

Back Neck Facing
Cut 1 Fabric
Cut 1 Interfacing

Front Facing
Cut 2 Fabric
Cut 2 Interfacing

Use the basic front and back bodice and sleeve block draft patterns as a foundation for the following.

These basic block patterns have to be enlarged to allow the coat to be worn over other garments and to be fully lined if required. Below are suggested widths for the fastening wrap to be added to the centre front line:

3cm (11/8") to 4cm (11/2") for a single wrap for all sizes.
8cm (31/8") for a double-breasted wrap for sizes 2-4-6.

10cm (4") for a double-breasted wrap for sizes 8-10.
12cm (43/4") for a double-breasted wrap for sizes 12-14.

The sleeve pattern must be adjusted to fit easily into the enlarged coat block armhole. It must have extra width throughout its length and the wrist must be kept loose to enable it to be worn comfortably over other sleeves.

Basic coat block draft

This basic coat block pattern has been drafted to knee length. It can be shortened to any required length.

1. Place the centre front and back bodices approximately 8cm (31/8") apart with the chest A-B in line.
   Trace around these patterns.

Back

C-D Lower the centre back neck 0.5cm (1/4") and draw a line parallel to the neck edge to D on the shoulder line.

D-E Mark 2cm (3/4") out from the shoulder/armhole point to E and join to D for the new shoulder line.

C-F Mark the centre back coat length. Square out from F.

G-H Square out from line A-B through the centre of the dart to H on the hemline.

F-H Join.

B-J Lower the armhole 2cm (3/4") at B and move out 3cm (11/8") to J.

J-K Square down from J to K on the hemline and join to F.

E-J Reshape the armhole from E to J utilizing the armhole shape of the back bodice block pattern.

J-L Pivot line J-K out 4cm (11/2") to L for amount required.

F-L Join F-H-K-L for the back coat hemline.

Front

C-D Lower the centre front neck 0.5cm (1/4") and draw a line parallel to the neck edge to D on the shoulder line.

D-E Mark out 2cm (3/4") from the shoulder/armhole point to E and join to D for the new shoulder line.

C-F Mark the centre front coat length. Square out from F.

G-H Square out from line A-B through the centre of the dart to H on the hemline.

F-H Join.

B-J Lower the armhole 2cm (3/4") at B and out 3cm (11/8") to J.

E-J Reshape the armhole from E to J utilizing the armhole shape of the front bodice block pattern.

J-K Square down from J to K. Make this line the same length as J-K on the back coat draft to equalize the side seam length.

J-L Pivot line J-K out 4cm (11/2") to L or the amount required.

F-L Join F-H-K-L for the front coat hemline.

M-N Mark the width of the fastening wrap required out from centre front line C-F to M and N. Join.

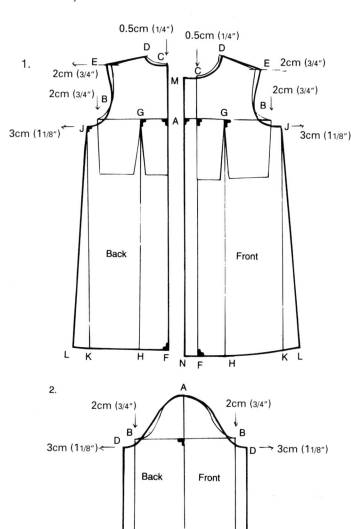

Sleeve

2. Trace around the basic sleeve block pattern placed on adjacent line A and B.
   Lower the armhole 2cm (3/4") at B and out 3cm (11/4") to D.
   Reshape the head of the sleeve from D to A on the front and back sleeve utilizing the block armhole shape.
   Mark the new sleeve seam from D to E parallel to B-C.
   Adjust the length of the sleeve as required.
   On the back sleeve wrist line F is half A-E and is down 0.5cm (1/4") for sizes 2-4-6 and 1cm (1/2") for sizes 8-10-12-14.
   On the front sleeve wrist line G is half A-E and is up 0.5cm (1/4") for sizes 2-4- 6 and 1cm (1/2") for sizes 8-10-12-14.
   Join E-F-A-G-E for the new wrist line.

Coats and jackets can be any length. Mark the required length down from C on the centre back neck.
Mark the position of any pockets or flaps required on the pattern.

3. Mark the position of the front and back neck facings.
   If a lining is required, then cut the pattern to the coat body and sleeve patterns, minus the front and back neck facings.

4. The lining patterns are cut to the finished length of the body and sleeve hems. When hemmed, the lining will be shorter than the coat.

5. Trace off the facing and interfacing patterns.
   Add seam and hem allowance and make corresponding balance marks.
   Mark the grain line on each pattern piece.
   Any collar and lapel shape can be adapted for the basic coat block.
   The basic tailored collar pattern can be drafted onto this pattern.

COAT PATTERNS

3.

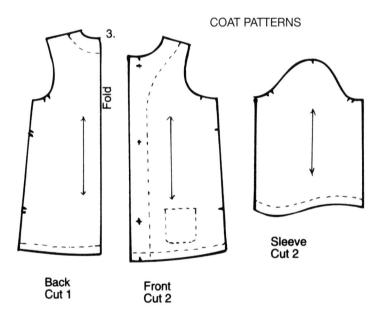

Back
Cut 1

Fold

Front
Cut 2

Sleeve
Cut 2

4.

LINING PATTERNS

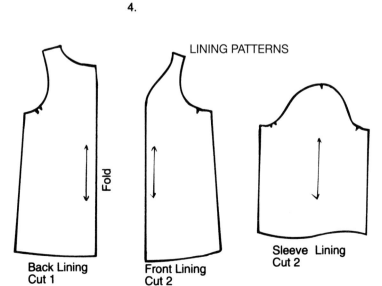

Back Lining
Cut 1

Fold

Front Lining
Cut 2

Sleeve Lining
Cut 2

5.

FACING PATTERNS

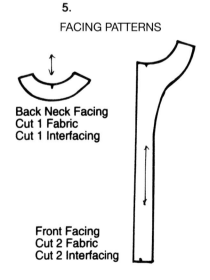

Back Neck Facing
Cut 1 Fabric
Cut 1 Interfacing

Front Facing
Cut 2 Fabric
Cut 2 Interfacing

Use the basic coat back, front and sleeve block draft patterns as a foundation for the following.

Raglan coat

This raglan coat pattern is more suitable for larger sizes. The basic tailored collar pattern can be drafted onto this coat pattern. Any collar and lapel shape can be adapted for the raglan coat.

Front and back

1. Trace around the basic front, back and sleeve coat block draft patterns.
   D-A Mark down 1.5cm (1/2") from D to A on the back neckline.
   D-B Mark down 1.5cm (1/2") from D to B on the front neckline.
   J-O Mark up 7cm (23/4") from J on the back armhole.
   J-P Mark 7cm (23/4") up from J on the front armhole.
   A-O Join with a curve.
   B-P Join with a curve.
   F-R Mark the centre back pleat length up from F.
        Square out approximately 6cm (23/8") from F-R to S-T.
        Join F-S-T-R for back pleat.

Sleeve

2. A-V Mark 1.25cm (1/2") from A to V on the back sleeve.
   A-W Mark 1.25cm (1/2") from A to W on the front sleeve.
   D-V Join with a curve.
   D-W Join with a curve.

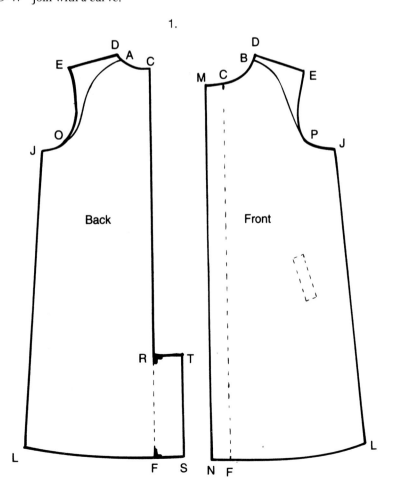

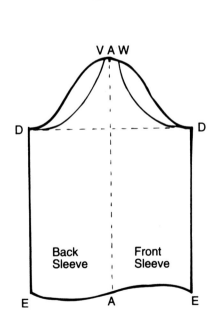

3. D-X   Taper the sleeve if required.

    D-Y   Taper the sleeve if required.

    X-Y   Reshape the wristline if the sleeve has been tapered.

    D-V   Slash from D to V and raise 4cm (11/2").

    D-W   Slash from D to W and raise 4cm (11/2").

    D-X   Reshape the sleeve seam to the elbow line which is midway between D and W on the back sleeve seam.

    D-Y   Reshape the sleeve seam to the elbow line which is midway between D and Y on the front sleeve seam.

4. A-O   Separate the back yoke section from the back pattern. Place this yoke section into position on the back sleeve with E raised 2cm (3/4") above V with point O on line D-V.

    B-P   Separate the front yoke section from the pattern. Place this yoke section into position on the front sleeve with E raised 2cm (3/4") above W with point P on line D-W.

    A-Z   Mark Z 2cm (3/4") below A. Join D to Z to form the shoulder dart in the front and back sleeve.

5. The one-piece sleeve has a long shoulder dart for fit.

6. For a two-piece sleeve, cut through line A-Z to separate the back and front sleeve.
    Seam D-Z-A from shoulder to wrist.

7. If a lining is required, then trace around the patterns minus the front and back neck facings.
    The lining patterns are cut to the finished length of the body and sleeve. When hemmed, the lining will be shorter than the coat.

8. Trace off the facing patterns.
    Add seam and hem allowance and make corresponding balance mark marks.
    Mark the grain line on each pattern piece.

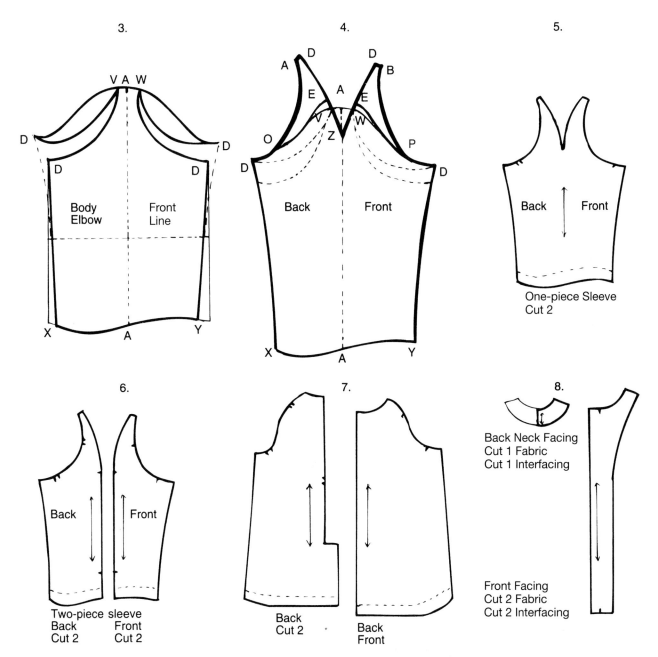

Use the basic front and back coat block draft patterns as a foundation for the following.

Princess line coat

This fitted style is more suitable for older girls in the larger sizes of 8-10-12-14.

1. Trace around the basic front and back coat block draft patterns. On the centre front line C-F, mark out the width of fastening required to M and N.
   Join M to N.
   Halve shoulder line D-E at O.
   Join O to G at the top of the dart with a slight curve.
   Join G to H on the hemline.
   Mark the amount of flare required each side of H for T and V.
   Join R to V and S to T making them the same length as X-H.
   For a more fitted waistline, mark in approximately 2cm (3/4") at W.
   Join J-W-L for the new side seam.

2. It is necessary to separate each pattern piece as the skirt panels overlap at the hemline.
   Trace around each pattern piece as indicated below.
   Centre back panel is C-F-T-S-G-O-D-C.
   Side back panel is O-G-R-V-L-W-J-E-O.
   Centre front panel is D-M-N-T-S-G-O-D.
   Side front panel is O-G-R-V-L-W-J-E-O.

3. Place the centre back line C-F on the fold.
   Mark and trace off the facing and interfacing patterns.
   If a lining is required, then mark and trace off this pattern.
   Add seam and hem allowance and make corresponding balance marks.
   Mark the grain line on each pattern piece.
   Use the basic coat sleeve block draft for this coat.
   Any collar and lapel shape can be adapted for the basic princess line coat.
   The basic tailored collar pattern can be drafted onto this pattern.

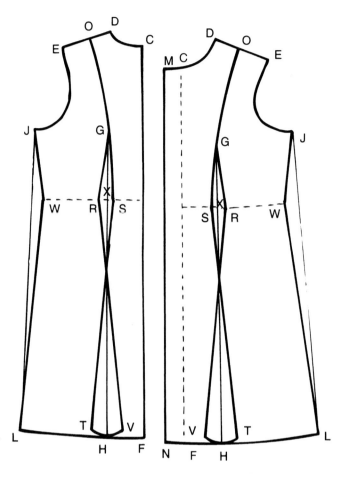

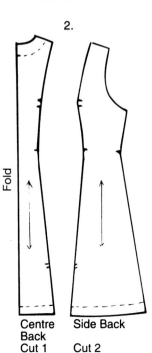

2.

Fold

Centre Back
Cut 1

Side Back
Cut 2

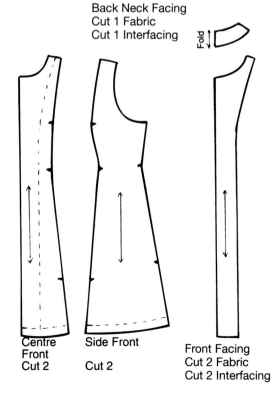

Back Neck Facing
Cut 1 Fabric
Cut 1 Interfacing

Fold

Centre Front
Cut 2

Side Front
Cut 2

Front Facing
Cut 2 Fabric
Cut 2 Interfacing

Basic tailored collar

Use any tailored jacket or coat draft pattern as a foundation for the following.

The width of the front fastening wrap must be added to the centre front pattern before drafting the collar.

1. Establish the rolling line of the lapel before drafting the collar.

2. A-B   Extend the shoulder line 2.5cm (1") to B.
   C-D   Mark down the depth of the rolling line required.
   B-D   Join.
   B-E   Extend line D-B to half the back neck measurement.
   E-F   Mark 1.25cm (1/2"). Square out each side of E.
   F-G   Join F to G on line E-D.
   F-H   From F mark out 3cm (11/8") for the depth of the collar stand.
   A-J   Mark 1.25cm (1/2").
   H-G   Join H to J and curve to G.
   F-K   Mark 4.5cm (13/4) for the width or fall of the collar. This must cover the collar stand when worn.
   K-L   Mark 0.5cm (1/4") above K for L.

   H-L   Join for the centre back of the collar.
   M-O   Shape the collar as required and join to L.

3. Trace and separate the collar M-G-J-H-L-O-M.
   G-F is the rolling line of the collar.
   G-D is the rolling line for the lapel. Add seam allowance and make corresponding balance marks.
   Mark the grain line on each pattern piece.

The collar and lapel can be of any shape. An alternative method of production is to draw the required collar and lapel shape on the bodice, then fold line B-D over to enable the style lines to be traced off.
The collar is then drafted the same way as the basic collar pattern.

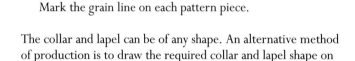

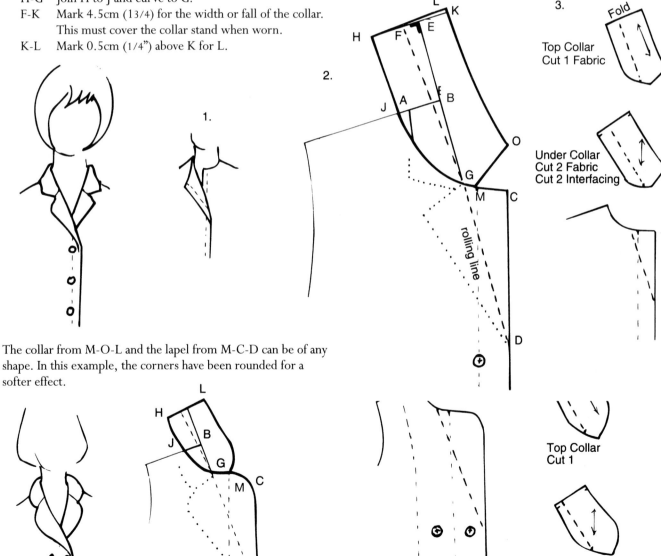

The collar from M-O-L and the lapel from M-C-D can be of any shape. In this example, the corners have been rounded for a softer effect.

Top Collar
Cut 1 Fabric

Under Collar
Cut 2 Fabric
Cut 2 Interfacing

Top Collar
Cut 1

Under Collar
Cut 2 Fabric
Cut 2 Interfacing

Pattern layout

After the patterns have been made, they must be laid out to establish the amount of fabric required for the garment.

The width of the fabric determines the pattern layout. A general rule is that the wider the fabric, the more economical the fabric usage.

All commercial printed paper patterns include diagrams for the pattern layouts most suitable for the different standard width fabric available.

The most economical method of laying out patterns on the fabric is to dovetail them together by placing them up and down the fabric.

When a fabric has a nap or pile, such as velvet, or is a one-way print, then the patterns must be laid facing one way only. More fabric will be used in this method and this additional amount must be calculated when ordering the material.

If the fabric is not a standard width or if the pattern has been altered or cut to special measurements, then the layout must be planned prior to purchase.

The diagrams on the page are a suggested pattern layout for the basic coat block draft on page 64 including fabric, interfacing and lining. The layout will vary according to the width of fabric used.

INTERFACING LAYOUT

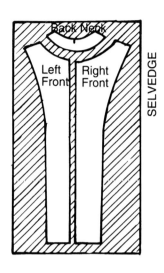

FABRIC LAYOUT

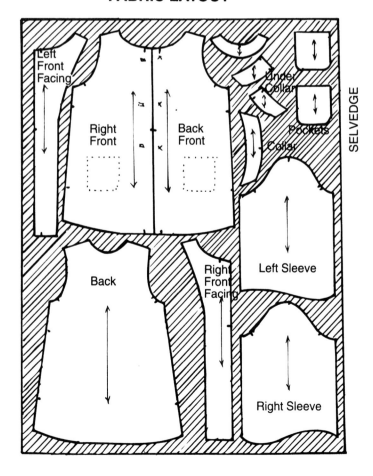

LINING LAYOUT

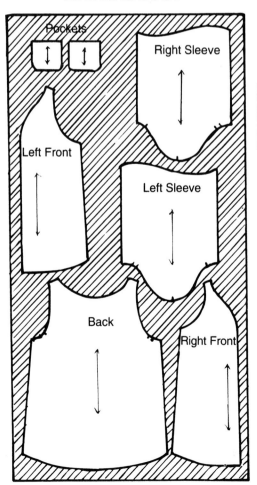

Cape patterns

Originally capes were short and only covered the upper part of the body. Cloaks were longer and gave added protection to the wearer. Cape is now the accepted word for any length of sleeveless covering falling from the neck.

Use either the basic front and back bodice or coat block draft patterns as a foundation for the following.

Flared cape

1. Square out from A on the centre back line to B at the armhole point.
   From C on the front armhole draw a line parallel to the waistline at D on the centre front.

2. Place the front and back bodices into position with the shoulder points together at E.
   Pivot the front bodice so B-C is half A-B.
   Join with a curve. G is half B-C.
   Draw a line from E through G for the side seam.
   Measure the back neck length from H to J.
   Mark lines G-K and D-L the same length as A-J.
   Join J-K-L with a curve for the hemline.
   For a well fitted shoulder line mark M 4cm (1 1/2") down from E and join to N and O for the shoulder dart.

3. Add seam and hem allowance and make corresponding balance marks.
   Mark the grain line on each pattern piece.
   The cape can be fully lined or faced around the neck and down the centre front.

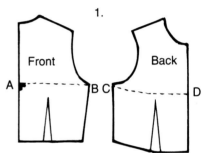

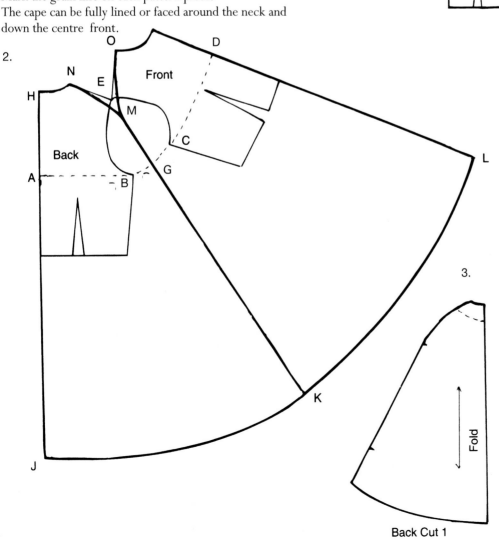

Half-circle cape

1. Square from A on the centre back line to B at the armhole point. From C on the front armhole draw a line parallel to the waistline D on the centre front.

2. Draw a right angle and place the front and back bodices in position with the shoulder points together at E.
   Draw a line from F through E for a side seam if required.
   Join B to C with a curve. G is half B-C.
   Measure the centre back length from H to J.
   G-K and D-L are the same length as A-J.
   Join J-K-L with a curve for the hemline.
   For a well fitted shoulder line, mark M 4cm (11/2") down from E and join to N and O for the shoulder dart.

3. Add seam and hem allowance and make corresponding balance marks.
   Mark the grain line on each pattern piece.
   This cape can be fully lined or faced around neck and down the centre front.
   It can be cut in one piece or seamed at the centre back.
   If a side seam is required, cut through line M-K.

4. One-piece cape.

Use either the basic front and back bodice or coat block draft patterns as a foundation for the following.

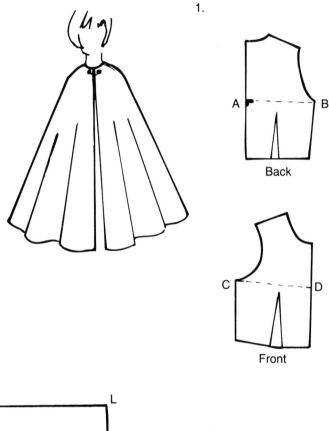

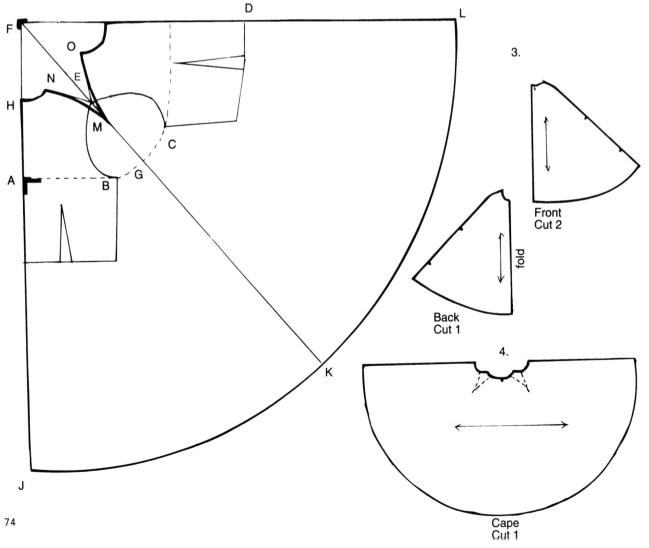

Use the basic front and back bodice or coat block draft patterns as a foundation for the following.

Poncho

This very simple square garment originated in South America. It can even be cut from a rug and can be any size from waist to floor length.
A comfortably sized poncho for a child will reach to the hand.

1. Measure from the nape of the back neck to the wrist.

2. Mark this measurement from A to B.
   Draw a line each side of A and place the centre front and back bodices on this line with the shoulder points together on line A-B.
   A-C and A-D are the same length as A-B.
   Mark the neckline from E to F, ensuring that it is sufficiently large for the garment to be comfortably pulled over the head.

3. Place line C-D on the fold.
   The neck can be bound or faced.
   The hemline is often fringed.
   Add the seam allowance.
   Mark the grain line on each pattern piece.

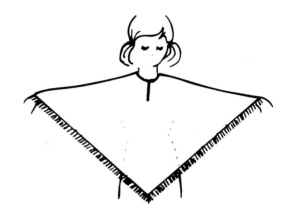

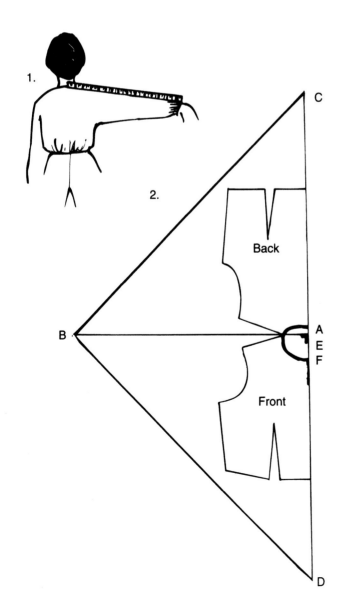

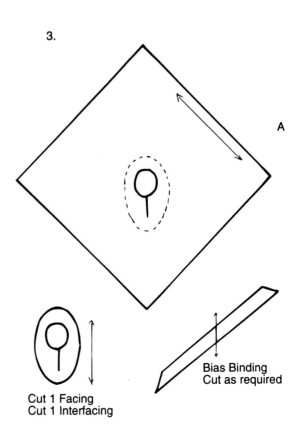

Cut 1 Facing
Cut 1 Interfacing

Bias Binding
Cut as required

Hood patterns

A hood can be a separate item or attached to the neckline of a garment. The latter is more practical for children as it cannot be lost. A hood generally has a drawcord or elastic around the face to keep it in place when worn.

These simple drafts should only be used as a basic pattern. The neck edge will have to be adjusted to fit the neckline of the garment.

Two main measurements are required to draft a hood pattern.

1. The over-the-head measurement is taken from the right neck edge of the garment over the top of the head to the left neck edge.

2. The around-the-head measurement is taken from midway between the right eye and the ear around the back of the head to the left side of the face.

The pattern should be cut and fitted in muslin or calico as a 'toile' prior to cutting out the fabric.

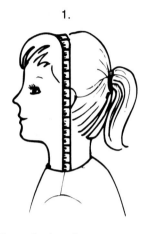

1.

Over-the-head measurement

2.

Around-the-head measurement

Basic hood

This hood is often referred to as a pixie hood because of the point at the back of the head.

A-B   Half the over-the-head measurement plus 6cm (2 3/4") ease.
       Square out from A and B.

A-C   Half the around-the-head measurement plus 2cm (3/4") ease.
       Square down to D and across to B.
       C-E is half C-D.
       Square across to K on A-B.

D-F   Mark in 4cm (1 1/2") to F.

F-G   Mark down 1.5cm (1/2") from F to G.

B-H   Mark down 4cm (1 1/2") from B.

B-I   Half B-D. Square up to J on line A-C.

G-H   Join C-I-H for the neck edge.

C-G   Join C-E-G for the back of head seam.

Place line A-C on the fold.

Make a casing hem for the face drawcord on line A-H.

Add seam and hem allowance and make corresponding balance marks.

Mark the grain lines on each pattern piece.

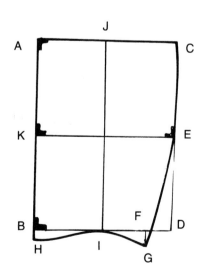

Use the basic hood draft as a foundation for the following.

Hood with a crown dart

C-L   1/3 of line C-A.
C-M   Equal to C-L.
      Square out from M and L to N.
      Place line A-L on the fold.
      Make a casing hem for the face drawcord on line A-H.
      Neck edge G-H can be gathered into the neck edge.
      Add seam allowance and make corresponding
      balance marks.
      Mark the grain line on each pattern piece.

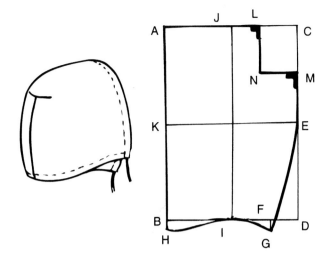

Rounded hood

A-O   Mark down 2cm (3/4") from A.
O-P   Mark 1.5cm (1/2") out from O-P.
H-P   Join H-K-P for new face edge.
G-P   Join G-E-J-P for the over-the-head seam.
      Add a casing hem for the face drawcord or cut a
      separate facing.
      Mark the grain line on each pattern piece.

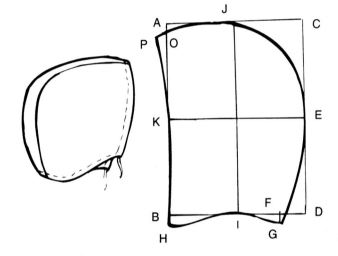

Fitted hood

This hood has a dart at the crown and the neckline to fit more
closely to the head and neck.
Align the hood dart with the shoulder seam of the garment and
take out half the dart required from each side of the shoulder
seam.
The neck dart length can be approximately 8cm (31/8") for sizes
2-4-6, 10cm (41/4") for sizes 8-10 and 12cm (43/4") for sizes
12-14.

Use the rounded hood as a foundation for the following.

C-M   Half C-E. Square out.
C-L   Equals line C-M. Sqare down for N.
C-N   Join. On line J-E mark 1cm (3/8") each side of line
C-N for crown dart.
N-R   Join.
N-S   Join.

Add a casing seam for the face drawcord or cut a
separate facing.
Add seam allowance and make corresponding
balance marks.
Mark the grain line on each pattern piece.

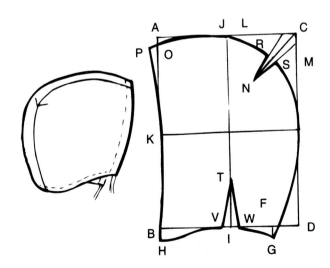

Pattern grading

Grading is the proportional increase or decrease of the block dart of a sample size pattern according to the standard body measurements used. It is the ideal method of adapting patterns for a growing child.

Grading is used extensively in garment manufacturing as it saves having to draft a different pattern for each size required.

A sample size for manufacturing in girlswear is usually size 10, indicated in the diagrams with a thicker line. The other lines indicate the smaller size 8 and the larger 12 and 14.

Grading can be used on any type of pattern, be it drafted or a purchased commercial printed paper pattern. The method is more suitable for the larger sizes of 8-10-12-14 and the measurements below are given for these sizes only.

If both sides of the pattern are identical, then half the pattern is used. If the pattern is not even, as with trouser patterns, then the full pattern must be used. Trace around the pattern prior to grading.

Mark inside the thick line for the smaller size 8 pattern and outside the thick line for the larger sizes of 12 and 14.

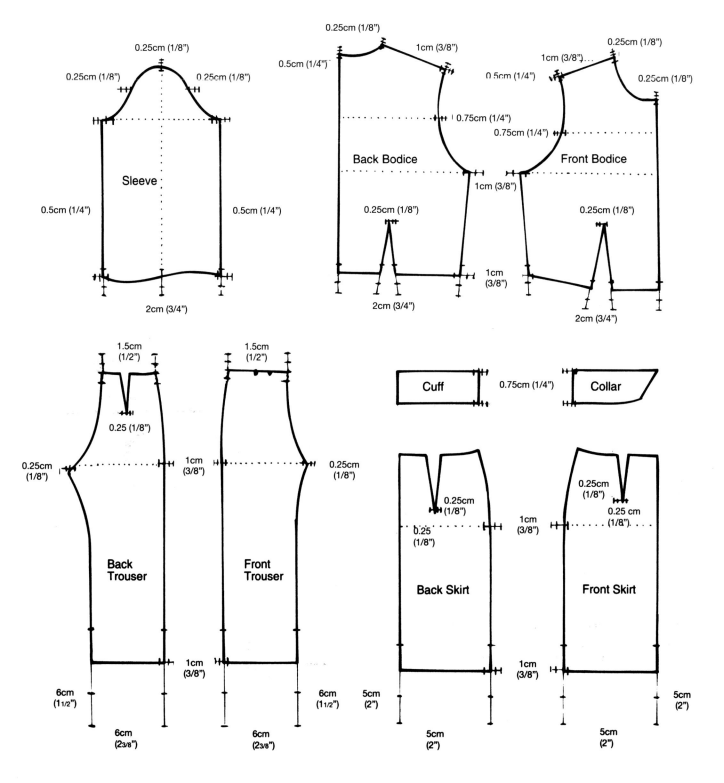

These diagrams illustrate where and how each pattern is 'graded'
to a smaller or larger size.

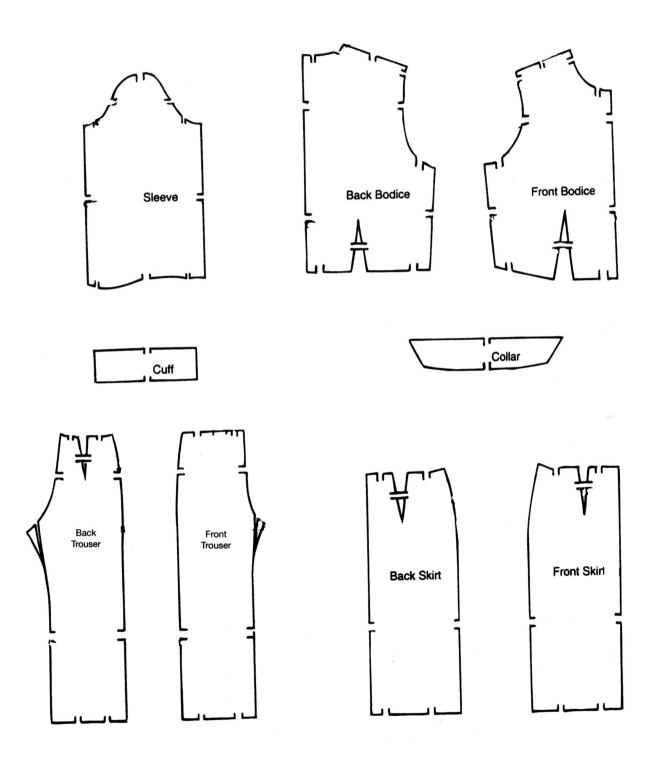

The pattern must be checked for accuracy when the size grading has been completed.
Place lines A-B and C-D together with the smallest size on top and largest size underneath. There should be an even grade between the sizes.

The following pattern gradings have size 8 on the top, with size 10 indicated by the thicker line, size 12 underneath and size 14 at the bottom of the stack.

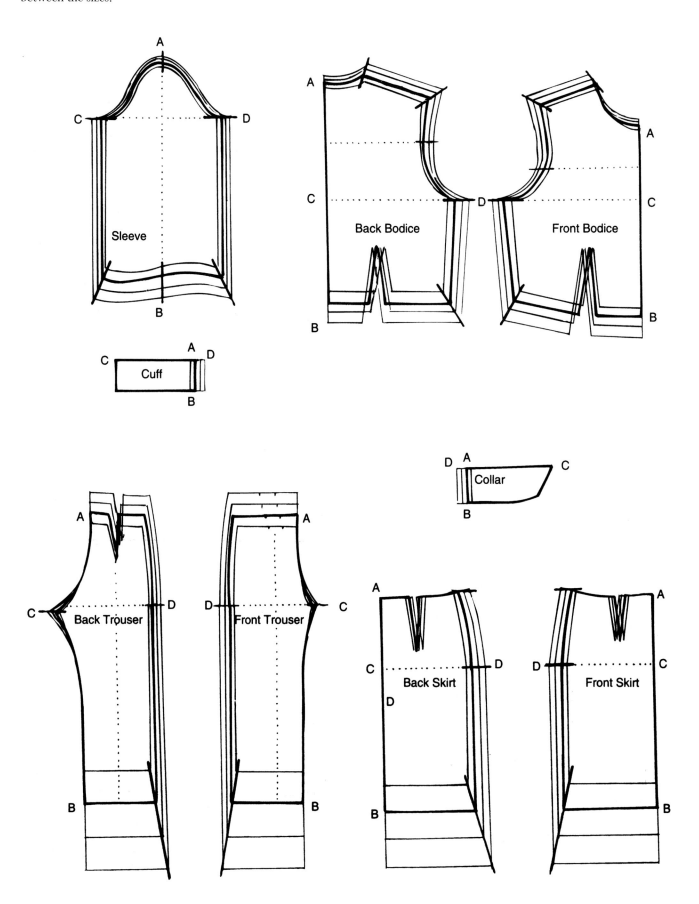

The principle of pattern grading is to keep the pattern in the same position for the size increase, regardless of the pattern shape. Common sense is all that is needed to work out the position for grading more complicated pattern shapes. The following examples illustrate this point. Skirt length grading is a matter of choice.

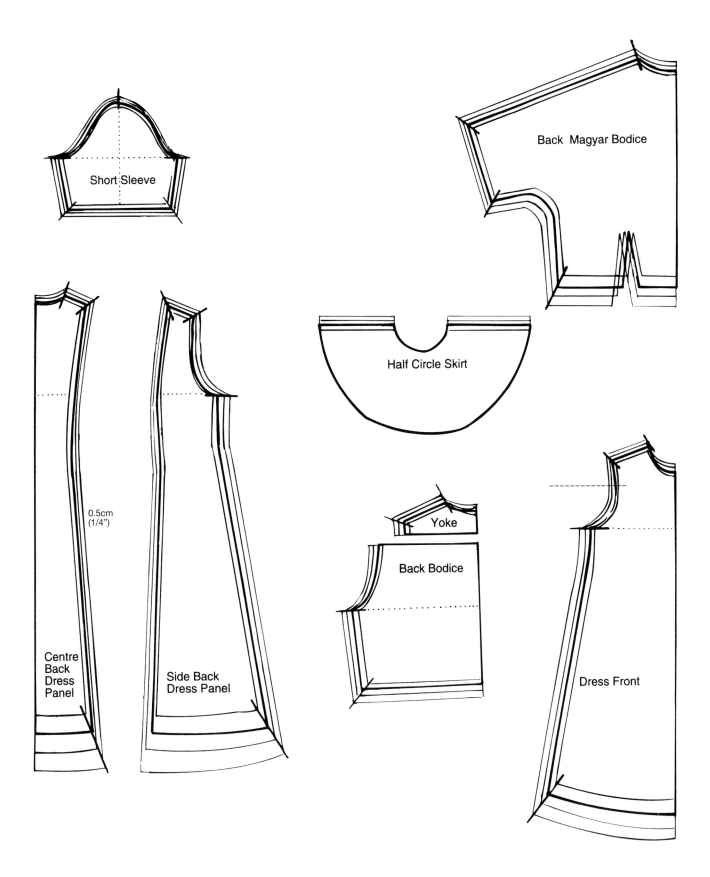

Short Sleeve

Back Magyar Bodice

Half Circle Skirt

0.5cm (1/4")

Centre Back Dress Panel

Side Back Dress Panel

Yoke

Back Bodice

Dress Front

Imperial measurement charts

Standard body measurement chart

	Children			Girls & Boys				Inches
Sizes	2	4	6	8	10	12	14	
1. Approximate age	2	4	6	8	10	12	14	Years
2. Height	36	42	47	51	55	59	63	Taken vertically from the crown of the head to the floor.
3. Chest	22	23 1/2	25	27	28 1/2	30	31 1/2	Taken around the body at the fullest part of the chest over the shoulder blades.
4. Waist	21 1/4	22	22 3/4	23 3/4	24 1/2	25 1/4	26	A comfortable measurement taken at the waistline.
5. Hips	22 1/2	24	25 1/2	27	28 1/2	30	31 1/2	Taken at the fullest part of the hipline.
6. Centre front	7 1/2	8 1/4	9	9 3/4	10 3/4	11 3/4	12 3/4	From base of front neck to waistline.
7. Across front	8 1/2	9	9 1/2	10 1/2	11 1/8	11 3/4	12 3/8	Approximately midway between the top and bottom of the armhole.
8. Centre back	9 1/4	10	10 3/4	11 1/2	12 1/2	13 1/2	14 1/2	From nape of back neck to waistline.
9. Across back	9	9 1/2	10	11	11 5/8	12 1/4	12 7/8	Over the shoulder blades, approximately midway between top and bottom of armhole.
10. Side seam	3 1/2	4 1/8	4 3/4	5 3/8	6	6 5/8	7 1/8	Up from waistline to approximately 1" below armpit.
11. Neck circumference	10	10 3/4	11 1/2	12 1/4	13	13 3/4	14 1/2	A loose measurement taken at the base of the neck.
12. Shoulder	2 3/4	3	3 1/4	3 1/2	3 3/4	4	4 1/4	From base of side neck to the shoulder point.
13. Over arm	14 1/2	16 1/2	18 1/2	21	23 1/2	26	28 1/4	From base of side neck to wrist with the arm bent.
14. Under arm	9 1/4	10 1/2	11 3/4	13	13 3/4	14 1/2	15 1/4	From the armhole to the wrist.
15. Upper arm	7	7 1/2	8	8 3/4	9	9 1/2	9 3/4	At fullest part of the bicep.
16. Body rise or crotch depth	8	8 3/4	9 1/2	10	10 1/2	11	11 1/2	Taken seated and measured from the side waist ot the seat, plus 1".
17. Waist to hip	4	4 1/2	5	5 1/2	6	6 1/2	7	From centre back waist to fullest part of the hipline.
18. Waist to knee	14	16	18	20	22	24	26	Taken from back waist to back of knee.
19. Waist height	22	25	28	31	34	37	40	From waist to floor.

82

Basic skirt block draft

	Children			Girls				Inches
Size	2	4	6	8	10	12	14	
A-B	11	13	15	17	19	21	23	Skirt length from back waist. Square out from A to B.
A-C	12 1/4	13 1/4	14 1/4	15 1/4	16 1/2	17 3/4	19	Half hip measurement plus ease. Square down to D.
A-E	4	4 3/4	5 1/2	6	6 1/4	6 3/4	7	Down from waist to hipline. Square across to E.
E-G	6	6 1/2	7	7 1/2	8	8 1/2	9	Half A-C minus 1/2″. Square up to H and down to F.
A-J	2 1/4	2 3/8	2 1/2	2 3/4	3	3 1/4	3 1/2	Equals B-U on back bodice.
J-L	3	3 1/4	3 1/2	3 3/4	4	4 1/4	4 1/2	Equals U-W on back bodice.
K-L	1/4	1/4	1/4	3/8	3/8	3/8	3/8	Mark up from K.
A-L								Join back waistline with a curve.
C-M	2 1/4	2 3/8	2 1/2	2 3/4	3	3 1/4	3 1/2	Equals E-V on the front bodice.
M-N	3 1/2	3 3/4	4	4 1/4	4 1/2	4 3/4	5	Equals V-X on the front bodice.
N-O	1/4	1/4	1/4	3/8	3/8	3/8	3/8	
C-O								Join with a curve for the front waistline.
L-G								Shape with a curve for the hipline.
O-G								Shape with a curve for the hipline.

The centre front and back pattern can be placed on the fold or seamed. Add seam allowance and make corresponding balance marks. Mark the grain line on each pattern piece.

This completes the basic front and back draft for sizes 2-4-6. Separate the front and back skirt through the side seam line G-F.

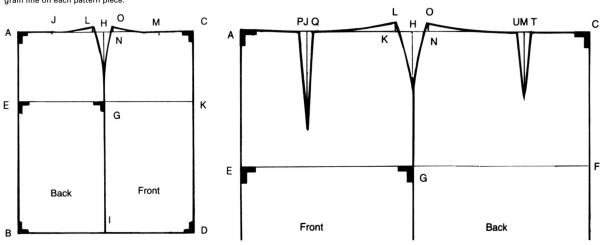

Basic skirt block draft with darts

	Children			Girls				
Size	2	4	6	8	10	12	14	Inches
J-R				4 1/2	4 3/4	5	5 1/4	Back length dart.
J-P				3/8	1/2	5/8	3/4	Half back dart width.
J-Q				3/8	1/2	5/8	3/4	Half back draft width. Join P-R-Q for back dart.
M-S				3 1/2	3 3/4	4	4 1/4	Front dart length.
M-T				3/8	1/2	5/8	3/4	Half front dart width.
M-U				3/8	1/2	5/8	3/4	Half front dart width. Join T-S-U for front dart.

This completes the construction of the basic skirt draft which is used as a foundation for the other skirt styles.
Separate the front and the back skirt at the side seam line G-F.

The centre front and back can be placed on the fold or seamed. Add seam allowance and make corresponding balance marks. Mark the grain line on each pattern piece.

Basic bodice block draft

	Children			Girls & Boys				Inches
Size	2	4	6	8	10	12	14	
A-B	9 1/4	10	10 3/4	11 1/2	12 1/2	13 1/2	14 1/2	Centre back length. Square across from A and B.
A-C	12 3/4	13 1/2	14 1/4	15	15 3/4	16 1/2	17 1/4	Half chest measurement plus ease. Square down from C for centre front line.
C-D	1 7/8	2	2 1/4	2 3/8	2 1/2	2 3/4	2 5/8	Front neck depth. Square out from D.
D-E	7 1/2	8 1/4	9	9 3/4	10 3/4	11 3/4	12 3/4	Centre front line.
B-F	3 1/2	4 5/8	4 3/4	5 1/2	6	6 1/2	7	Side seam length. Square out from F to G on centre front line D-E.
F-H	6	6 1/4	6 3/4	7	7 1/2	8	8 1/2	Half back chest measurement plus ease and minus 1/2". Square down from H.
H-H/1	3 1/2	4	4 3/4	5 1/2	6	6 1/2	7	Equals B-F side seam length.
A-I	2 5/8	2 3/4	2 7/8	3	3 1/4	3 1/2	3 3/4	Half A-F.
I-J	4 1/2	4 3/4	5	5 1/2	5 3/4	6	6 1/2	Half across back measurement. Square down to K on line F-H.
K-K/1	3/4	3/4	3/4	1	1	1	1	Bisect angle J-K-H.
D-L	1 5/8	1 3/4	1 7/8	2	2 1/8	2 1/4	2 3/8	Half D-G.
L-M	4 1/4	4 1/2	4 3/4	5	5 1/2	6	6 1/4	Half across front measurement. Square down to N on line G-H.
N-N/1	1/2	1/2	1/2	3/4	3/4	1	1	Bisect angle M-N-H.
A-O	3/8	3/8	3/8	1/2	1/2	1/2	1/2	Back neck height. Square out from O.
O-P	1 7/8	2	2 1/8	2 3/8	2 1/2	2 5/8	2 3/4	
A-P								Join back with a curve.
C-Q	1 3/4	2	2 1/4	2 3/8	2 1/2	2 5/8	2 3/4	Equals O-P on back neck. Square down to R.
C-R								Join.
R-R/1	1/2	1/2	1/2	1	1	1	1	
D-Q								Join front neck shape with a curve.
I-I/1	1	1	1	1	1	1	1	
I-Q								Join for front shoulder slope.
L-P								Join for front shoulder slope.
P-S	2 3/4	3	3 1/4	3 1/2	3 3/4	4	4 1/4	Back shoulder length.
Q-T	2 3/4	3	3 1/4	3 1/2	3 3/4	4	4 1/4	Front shoulder length.
S-T								Join S-J-K/1-H-N/1-M-T for the armhole with a good curve.
B-U	2 1/4	2 3/8	2 1/2	2 3/4	3	3 1/4	3 1/2	Square out from B for back waistline.
E-V	2 1/4	2 3/8	2 1/2	2 3/4	3	3 1/4	3 1/2	Square out from E for front waistline.
H/1-W	3/8	3/8	3/8	3/8	3/8	3/8	3/8	
H/1-X	3/8	3/8	3/8	3/8	3/8	3/8	3/8	
H-W	3 1/2	4	4 3/4	5 1/4	6	6 1/2	7	Join.
H-X	3 1/2	4	4 3/4	5 1/4	6	6 1/2	7	Join.

On the front bodice armhole measure in 1 1/2" from
H for the position of the front sleeve balance mark.
On the back bodice armhole measure in 1 1/2" and 2"
from H for the position of the back sleeve balance marks.
Separate the front and back bodices at H-Y and H-X. This
completes the basic front and back bodice block draft for
children 2-4-6 and girls and boys 8-10-12-14.
The centre front and back can be placed on the fold
or seam.
Add seam allowance and make corresponding
balance marks.
Mark the grain line on each pattern piece.

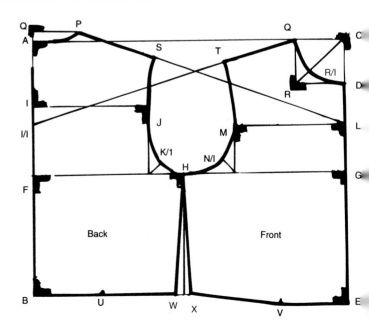

Basic bodice block draft with drafts

Size			Girls					Inches
	2	4	6	8	10	12	14	
U-Y				4 1/2	4 3/4	5	5 1/4	Back dart length.
U-U/1				3/8	1/2	5/8	3/4	Half back dart width.
U-U/2				3/8	1/2	5/8	3/4	Half back dart width. Join U/1-Y-U/2 for back dart.
V-Z				5	5 1/4	5 1/2	5 3/4	Front dart length.
V-V/1				3/8	1/2	5/8	3/4	Half front dart width.
V-V/2				3/8	1/2	5/8	3/4	Half front dart width. Join V1/Z-V/2 for front dart.

On the front bodice armhole measure 1 1/2" in from H for the position of
the front sleeve balance mark.
On the back bodice armhole measure 1 1/2" and 2" in from H for the position
of the back sleeve balance marks.
Separate the front and back bodices at H.
This completes the basic front and back bodice block draft.
After separating the back bodice at H-W and front bodice at H-X, place the
shoulders together at the neck point to ensure that there is a smooth curve
to the neckline.
The centre front and back can be placed on the fold or the seams.
Add seam allowance and make corresponding balance marks.
Mark the grain line on each pattern piece.

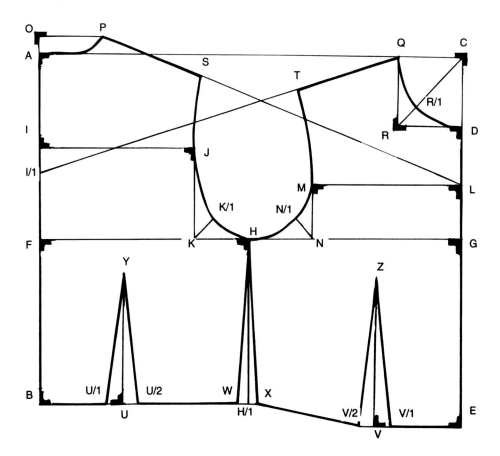

Basic sleeve block draft

Sizes	Children			Girls & Boys				Inches
	2	4	6	8	10	12	14	
A-B	3 1/2	3 3/4	4	4 1/4	4 1/2	4 3/4	5	Sleeve crown height. Square across from A and B.
B-C	9 1/4	10 1/2	11 3/4	13	13 3/4	14 1/2	15 1/4	Underarm length. Square across from C.
A-D	8 1/2	9	9 1/2	10 1/4	10 5/8	11	11 3/8	Bicep measurement plus ease. Square down from D and E.
B-F								Square across to D-E.
A-G	4 1/4	4 1/2	4 3/4	5	5 1/4	5 1/2	5 3/4	Half A-D. Square down to H on line C-E.
A-I	1	1 1/8	1 1/4	1 3/8	1 1/2	1 5/8	1 3/4	Approximately 1/3 of line A-B. Square across to line D-F.
B-J	1	1 1/8	1 1/4	1 3/8	1 1/2	1 5/8	1 3/4	Approximately 1/3 of line A-B. Square across to line D-F.
I-K	2 5/8	2 3/4	2 7/8	3	3 1/8	3 1/4	3 1/2	
J-L	1 7/8	2	2 1/8	2 1/4	2 3/8	2 1/2	2 5/8	
K-M	3 1/2	3 3/4	4	4 1/4	4 1/2	4 3/4	5	
L-N	5	5 1/4	5 1/2	5 3/4	6	6 1/4	6 1/2	
B-F								Join B-L-K-G-M-N-F for sleeve head shape.
C-P	2 1/8	2 1/4	2 3/8	2 1/2	2 5/8	2 3/4	2 7/8	1/4 line C-E.
E-O	2 1/8	2 1/4	2 3/8	2 1/2	2 5/8	2 3/4	2 7/8	1/4 line C-E.
Q-O	1/4	1/4	1/4	3/8	3/8	3/8	3/8	Mark down for back wristline.
P-R	1/4	1/4	1/4	3/8	3/8	3/8	3/8	Mark down for back wristline.
C-E								Join C-R-H-Q-E for wrist line.

For the front sleeve balance mark measure up 1 1/2" from E on the front sleeve head.

For the back sleeve balance measure up 1 1/2" and 2" from F on the back sleeve head.

Add seam allowance and make corresponding balance marks.

Mark the grain line on each pattern piece.

The wrist edge of the sleeve can be finished with a hem, facing, binding, cuff or elasticised.

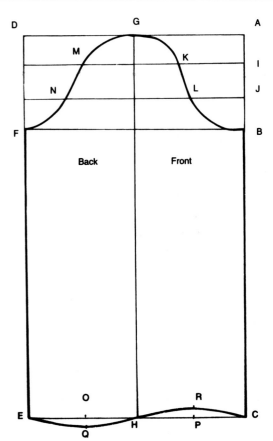

Tapered sleeve

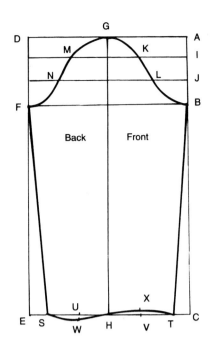

	Girls & Boys				Inches
Size	8	10	12	14	
E-S	1	1	1	1	
C-T	1	1	1	1	Equals E-S.
F-S					Join.
B-T					Join.
H-U	2	2 1/8	2 1/4	2 3/8	Half H-S.
H-V	2	2 1/8	2 1/4	2 3/4	Half H-T.
U-W	3/8	3/8	3/8	3/8	Mark down for back wristline.
V-X	3/8	3/8	3/8	3/8	Mark up for front wristline.
S-T					Join S-W-H-X-T for the wristline.

Add seam allowance and make corresponding balance marks.
Mark the grain line on each pattern piece.

Culottes or divided skirt

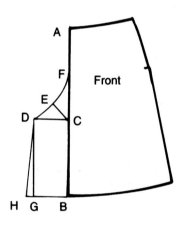

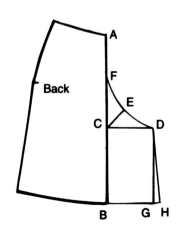

Size	8	10	12	14	Inches
Front					
A-B	16	18	20	22	Required skirt length.
A-C	10 1/4	10 5/8	11	11 3/8	Body rise or crotch depth. Square across from C.
C-D	3 1/2	3 3/4	4	4 1/4	1/8 hip measurement. Bisect angle A-C-D.
C-E	2	2 1/8	2 1/4	2 3/8	Half C-D plus 1/4".
C-F	7	7	7	7	On line A-B.
D-F					Join D-E-F with a curve for the fork section. Square down from D to G.
G-H	3/8	3/8	3/8	3/8	Pivot out 3/4" from G to H. Join H to D. D-H equals B-C.
Back					
A-B	16	18	20	22	Required skirt length.
A-C	10 1/4	10 5/8	11	11 3/8	Body rise or crotch depth. Square across from C.
C-D	5 1/4	5 1/2	5 3/4	6	1/8 hip measurement plus 1/2"
C-E	2 1/2	2 5/8	2 3/4	2 7/8	Half C-D.
C-F	3/4	3/4	3/4	3/4	On line A-B.
D-F					Join D-E-F with a curve for the fork section. Square down from D to G.
G-H	3/8	3/8	3/8	3/8	Pivot out 3/4" from G to H. Join H to D. D-H equals B-C.

Basic trouser block draft

	Children							Inches
Size	2	4	6	8	10	12	14	
A-B	18	21	24	27	30	33	36	Side seam length from back waist to ankle. Square out each side of A and B.
A-C	4	4 3/4	5 1/2	6	6 1/4	6 3/4	7	Waist to hip. Square out each side of C.
A-D	7 1/2	8 1/4	9	9 3/4	10 1/2	11 1/2	2 1/4	Body rise plus ease. Square out each side of D.
D-E	5	6 1/4	7 1/2	8 1/2	9 3/4	11	12 1/4	Knee line half D-B. Square out.
A-F	6	6 1/2	7	7 3/4	8 1/4	8 3/4	9 1/2	1/4 hip measurement plus ease. Square down to G and H.
H-I	1 1/8	1 3/8	1 1/2	1 3/4	2	2 1/4	2 1/2	
H-H/1	7/8	1	1 1/8	1 1/4	1 1/2	1 3/4	1 5/8	Bisect angle G-H-I.
F-I								Join F-G-H/1-I for centre front seam.
A-J	6	6 1/2	7	7 3/4	8 1/4	8 3/4	9 1/2	1/4 hip measurement plus ease. Square down L and M.
J K	1/4	1/4	1/2	1/2	3/4	3/4	1	Back seam suppression. Join to L.
M-N	2 3/4	2 7/8	3	3 1/4	3 1/2	3 3/4	4	
M-M/1	1 1/8	1 3/8	1 1/2	1 3/4	1 7/8	2	2 1/8	Bisect angle L-M-N.
N-N/1	1/4	1/4	1/4	3/8	3/8	3/8	3/8	Mark down from N.
K-N/1								Join K-L-M/1-N/1 for centre back seam.
E-O	6 1/4	6 3/4	7	8	8 3/4	9 1/2	10 1/4	1/2 knee measurement plus ease. Square down to Q.
E-P	6 1/4	6 3/4	7	8	8 3/4	9 1/2	10 1/4	1/2 knee measurement plus ease. Square down to R.

The above draft is ideal for the smallest sizes (2-4-6) as it is not necessary to have either side seams or waist darts due to the slightness of the variation between the waist and hip measurements.

The trousers can be cut in two pieces or, if a side seam is required, cut through line A-B.

This draft can be used for all sizes where elasticised waistline is required for comfort such as in track suit pants and pyjamas.

Add seam allowance and make corresponding balance marks.

Mark the grain line on each pattern piece.

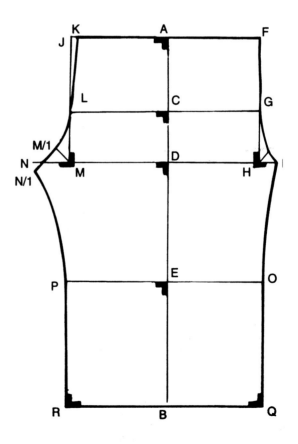

Basic trouser block draft with darts

	Children			Girls & Boys				Inches
Size	2	4	6	8	10	12	14	
K-K/1				3/8	1/2	5/8	3/4	Extend line L-K above line J-F. Join K to a with a curve.
A-A/1				1/8	3/8	1/2	3/4	Mark each side of A. Join to C with a curve.
K/1-S				2 7/8	3 1/8	3 3/8	3 5/8	Join with a curve.
S-U				1/4	3/8	1/2	5/8	Half back dart width.
S-V				1/4	3/8	1/2	5/8	Half back dart width.
S-T			Girls	4 1/4	4 3/4	5	5 1/2	Back dart length. Join U-T-V for back dart.
			Boys	3 3/4	4	4 1/2	5	Back dart length. Join U-T-V for back dart.
F-W				2 1/2	2 3/4	3	3 1/2	
W-X				1 1/4	1 1/2	1 3/4	2	Front tuck width.
	for front darts only			**Girls**				
W-Y				1/2	5/8	3/4	7/8	Half front dart width.
Y-X				1/2	5/8	3/4	7/8	Half front dart width.
Y-Z				3 1/2	3 3/4	4	4 1/4	Front dart length. Join W-Z-X for front dart.

Separate the draft at line A-B for the side seam.
Add seam allowance and make corresponding balance
marks. Mark grain lines.

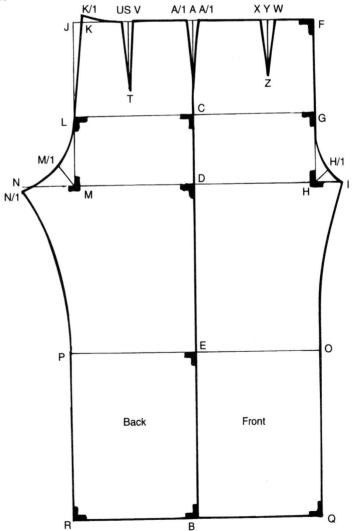